FIBERARTS DESIGN
BOOK FIVE

· · · · · · ·

FIBERARTS

DESIGN

BOOK

FIVE

Commentaries by
**Jan Janeiro &
Jack Lenor Larsen**

Edited by
**Ann Batchelder
& Nancy Orban**

Cover: Detail of Tracy Krumm's Her Sorrow, Unmasked.
Photo: courtesy Hibberd-McGrath Gallery, Breckenridge, Colorado.

Details on previous page:
Top, Ruth Manning. Bottom, David Brackett.
Opposite page: Mitsuko Tarui.

Published in 1995 by Lark Books
50 College Street
Asheville, North Carolina, U.S.A. 28801
Copyright © 1995, Lark Books

Art Director: Kathleen Holmes
Editors: Ann Batchelder and Nancy Orban
Production: Kathleen Holmes and Elaine Thompson

Library of Congress Cataloging-in-Publication Data
   Fiberarts design book five : commentaries / by Jan Janeiro and Jack Lenor Larsen.
       p.   cm.
   ISBN 0-937274-86-0
   1. Textile crafts.   2. Fiberwork.   I. Janeiro, Jan.   II. Larsen, Jack Lenor.
   TT699-F525   1995
   746--dc20   95-6604
                                                              CIP

10 9 8 7 6 5 4 3 2 1

Printed by Oceanic Graphic Printing in Hong Kong

ISBN 0-937274-86-0

CONTENTS

Foreword   7

Reflections on
Contemporary Design   8

Evolution and Trends
in the Fiber Arts Movement   11

Surface Design   17

Wearables   47

Needlework   71

Two Dimensions   87

Three Dimensions   117

Diversions   141

Tapestry   151

Paper & Felt   189

Quilts   203

Index   235

Annemarie Buchmann-Gerber

Akemi Nakano Cohn

FOREWORD

THIS FIFTH EDITION of The FIBERARTS Design Book features work completed in the period between 1991 and 1994. Its publication coincides with the 20th anniversary of FIBERARTS Magazine.

In honor of this anniversary we invited two prominent figures in the textile field to comment on the development of contemporary fiber art: Jan Janeiro, who skillfully weaves her own art career with that of observer and critic, and Jack Lenor Larsen, who has successfully combined a clear artistic vision and a savvy business sense with an appreciation for contemporary fiber.

It has now been two decades since the first generation of contemporary artists interested in handcrafts threw their first pot, wove a shawl, made a walnut box, strung a necklace or cobbled a pair of sandals. These same enthusiasts were responsible for launching a number of craft magazines, swelling the attendance at local, regional, and national craft fairs, filling workshops and craft schools, and helping countless craft supply shops get their start. Thousands of them wandered off into other pursuits, taking with them an appreciation for what is required to create a handsome craft piece. We like to think they are now the major buyers of fine craft.

In fiber art, as with other mediums, many artists continued to develop their skills but could only afford to do so on a part-time basis. Others who chose to make fiber their life's work began honing their artistic visions. They also started teaching, establishing fiber art programs at universities, and exhibiting their work at national and international levels. FIBERARTS Magazine has been part of this evolution and has reflected the artistic and philosophical trends in the fiber field.

Every few years it is a rewarding and enlightening experience to watch this growth through each new edition of the Design Book. In recent years surface design exploded onto the scene, for example. There has also been a growing respect for traditional techniques, more forceful uses of color, an increase in combining mediums, a greater narrative quality in many works, an exploration of cloth as metaphor, and an expanding international scope in the fiber field.

Over 6,000 entries from 34 countries were submitted for this Design Book competition. The work was chosen based on three criteria: artistic integrity, technical expertise, and innovative ideas (in short, "we liked it"). For the sake of organization, the pieces are loosely grouped into chapters.

In this fifth edition of the Design Book we see the control, confidence, and technical mastery of the generation that has artistically matured over the past 20 years coupled with the vibrant work of a new generation that is now joining the field. We are dedicated to encouraging both the professional artist and the talented amateur. It is in this spirit that we celebrate the 20th anniversary of FIBERARTS Magazine and invite you to explore this exciting and evolving art form.

The FIBERARTS Staff

REFLECTIONS ON CONTEMPORARY DESIGN

BY JACK LENOR LARSEN

As THIS CENTURY (and, indeed, millennium) so rapidly races to a finish, I have concerns for the future of design and architecture, the crafts movement as a whole, and aspects of textile arts within that movement.

Without doubt, I am nostalgic for the fervor with which certain visionaries faced up to the end of the last century, especially in their dynamic expressions of Art Nouveau in anticipation of a "century of progress." From this distance, it seems they possessed hope—and, perhaps, higher expectations than we do today. In several languages there was much talk about "spirit of progress" and of a vision with which we would finally harness industry—not to simply produce more goods for wider markets (and enrich a growing number of individuals in the process), but to resolve problems of distance through speed and communications, overcome disease through scientific breakthroughs, and fix crowded cities by building tall towers. Even peace seemed assured. Literally and figuratively, there was electricity in the air as a European-dominated world settled in for *la belle epoch*.

While the technologies of science and industry were destined to be the servant of all work, there was also a raging new interest in handcrafts found in prehistoric archeology and ethnography as well as brave new expressions in the fine arts of ceramics, metal, and glass. It was an exciting time, when the whole 20th century was young, and the New World its brash young star. When Americans were so hell-bent on catching up with Europe we passed that older culture in such major arenas as electricity, telecommunication, mass production, skyscrapers, and department stores.

In Gertrude Stein's *Brewsie and Willie*, two American G.I.s discuss America from a WWII battlefield in France. Willie says, "America is the oldest country in the world." When Brewsie asks why, Willie responds, "Because we entered the 20th century *first*." Oh, to be so young and cocky, not yet burdened with disillusion and global responsibility!

Just as exciting was the triumph of Modernism which had incubated all through the '20s and '30s, primarily in Europe. Modernism exploded after WWII in North America, where industry and the economy were then not only intact, but in high gear. We Modernists thought we *knew*. We believed that our new ratio-

Ethel Stein's A Portrait, 1994; *draw loom controlled Lampas weave (combination of two structures) with dyed mercerized cotton; 60 by 36 inches. Photo: James Karales.*

Top: Ana Lisa Hedstrom's resist dyed silks. Photo: Barry Shapiro.

Bottom: Marc Leuthold's Carved White Wheel, Side A, *1993; carved ceramic stoneware; 28 inches diameter. Photo: courtesy the artist; collection of Jack Lenor Larsen.*

nalism, stepping over traditional conventions to do everything the right way (if not the Wright way), would create new art, architecture, and "good design for Everyman."

And, of course, the honest craftsman would be part of it all. We were then, in the '40s and '50s, Designer Craftsmen as proof of our allegiance to modern design and our indifference to the prewar past.

What happened? Acceptance. The broad, popular embrace of the corporate establishment did, in some ways, create a golden age. If there are too few architectural milestones, we gained, instead, a great deal of tall real estate with the stripped-down, no-nonsense frugality of Modernism. As in all successful revolutions, the militants somehow become an establishment—or in this case, allied with *the* Establishment. The point is, Modernists thought they had won! And perhaps they did, but by and large these one-time eggheads were bought off by heady talk of 50 stories or 50 millions.

So it remains today for product design in general: the race for market share keeps the more able designers preoccupied with "urgencies of the new," and distracted from *real* solutions to real needs—which would be *really* new. Interestingly enough, the consumer market, particularly in home furnishings, long ago bolted *away* from Modernist style to pluralist approaches—reasonably searching for personal expressions on one hand, or an editorial moment on the other. To everyone's credit, Modernist freedoms persist through most of this parade of styles: furniture arrangements tend to relate to conversation groups, and, at least for now, informality persists. Integration of indoor/outdoor living spaces and more openness to color and pattern prevail.

By and large, today's furnishings are less focused on current design than at midcentury. Most recently built spaces are blandly empty with monotonous surfaces, lacking architectural detail or enriching expressions of materials and structure or any aspect of personal identity. In an increasingly impersonal world, how do the habitants create a safe harbor that feels like home and speaks of personal interests?

Collecting, surely, is the most popular solution—we have never seen such an array of collectibles. Show houses and house tours are at an all-time high. So are antique shows and art and craft galleries. Craft collecting, of course, has the most charm, the broadest spectrum, and the largest potential. Offerings include creditable craft for every purse, with and without function, in a range of styles and a gamut of media, scaled from furniture to finger rings. Responsive producers can expand their offerings to accommodate the market. The individuality of the artists is also part of the appeal: their nonconformity is legendary.

In the last decade we witnessed a major flare-up regarding questions of art versus craft, and one doubts that any major reso-

lution will occur soon. To the question: Is it art or craft? the answer could be neither. All too much shown in fairs and galleries has great flaws in quality or concept. In America, in particular, ambitious new artists attempt to work beyond their skills or experience. Such work is usually unresolved in terms of composition or presence. Work in fabric media seems particularly problematic. Sure, there are just as many unresolved paintings, but dismissing them seems easier. Most painters know their work will not "stand inspection" on its craft alone. They are also more willing to paint dozens, even hundreds, of canvases before opportunity to show them. This, I feel, is a key factor: all of us are so infatuated with new work as to have little perspective on its worth.

The fairly recent notion that artists (in all media) should market their art and "compete in the marketplace" has led to hype on one hand and turned heads on another. East European weavers I knew best in the '60s (such as Magdalena Abakanowicz) were willing to spend 20 years developing a technique, then a year on a single piece. This gave their work great quality.

Fabric techniques, of course, are usually slow in execution. A potter or glass blower can quickly repeat the same form dozens, even hundreds, of times—just as Picasso did his drawings. Skill and development of form are perfected in the process; so is the perception of the maker. Those of us who work in fiber seldom develop "sketch techniques" with which to hone our craft. Instead, we spend much time (and, too often, not enough) on statements too valuable to put aside.

Sample making works well for those of us who design. The Scots tapestry weaver Archie Brennan, now working in New York City, achieves something similar with woven miniatures only a few inches on a side. In this way he can perfect form as well as attempt changes in yarn surface or color value. He learns in the process, and those of us lucky enough to own one of Brennan's small works are the richer for it.

What is the hallmark of work that "is neither art nor craft"? Presumption, I believe. That which presumes to be more than it is can never be beautiful. Works too large, too ambitious have no humility. Those that are useful have at least that humble virtue— often more. Those that are useless either *are* art or something much less. Any crafted artifact, however useful, is potentially art. When we recall that the most popular art shows in recent times— Tutankhamen, "The Treasures of Dresden," as well as the major Chinese and Japanese exhibitions—were dominated by works in craft media, the point becomes clearer.

Top: Ana Lisa Hedstrom's Silk Coat, 1994; *resist dyed and pieced.*
Photo: Kim Harrington.

Bottom: Archie Brennan's At A Window-XII, 1992; *tapestry with mixed yarn weft and cotton warp; 35 by 27 inches. Photo: courtesy the artist.*

Evolution and Trends in the Fiber Arts Movement

BY JAN JANEIRO

Tom Lundberg's Holding Pattern, 1992; *embroidery on velvet; 12-3/4 by 12 3/4 inches. Photo: Colorado State University Photographic Services.*

BY THE MID-19TH CENTURY, textiles in the Western world were reduced to being either a mass-produced industrial product or a domestic craft. In the former case, textiles had become functional fabric and in the latter case, "women's work." Suddenly, it seemed, in the late-20th century an increasing number of trained artists were choosing to work with threads and looms to create work that exploded the myths of "mere" functionality, of maker-anonymity, and of domestic kitsch. The "new textiles" of the 1960s, which explored the limitations of traditional textile forms and techniques, declared that a new art form had been developed, and that, like painting and sculpture, textiles could be used as a medium expressive of individual emotions and ideas.

To appreciate the development of contemporary textile art since the '60s, one must return to the textile culture of the '40s and '50s. That was the last period in which there was, at least ostensibly, a unified vision of the role that textiles should play in a modern society. Shaped by a North American translation of the European Arts and Crafts Movement and early Modernist theories emanating from the recently defunct Bauhaus, textiles were wrapped in a mantle of "contemporary design."

Since William Morris's attempts to create handmade objects at a price that all could afford had failed, it was acknowledged that handweaving was unable to compete with its machine-produced progeny. The role of the textile designer was therefore to create "models for industry," those handwoven, hand-printed designs that were to be taken by textile mills and produced in great quantity at great speed.

As with most of the craft media, textiles merged a strong moral component, promulgated by Arts and Crafts reformer/advocates, with a strong functionalist component, originating from the theorizing of the Bauhaus and the Internationalist style of architecture that it had helped develop. Weavers and printers had accepted the responsibility of creating "artful" responses to the new pared-down interiors; they were to design the fabrics that would clothe the people and buildings of the developing industrial world. The "new" textile designer was to be an explorer of innovative materials, utilizing old technical structures to create new products that would meet the needs and reflect the reductivist aesthetic of the modern world. This seemed a worthy and realistic goal, and it received added impetus from the excitement of working with the "scientific" fibers and materials produced by a war industry now turned domestic. Working with industry gave the handweaver/designer the illusion of being on the "cutting edge" of modernity, of technological innovation.

Since decoration and pattern had become anathema to the modern spirit (or more appropriately, the modern "style"), textile designers worked within fixed limitations: color, texture, and structure were the boundaries of both their visual and technical vocabularies. In exhibits of contemporary design, textiles were the backdrop—just as they were in actual living and work spaces. They were the rugs upon which sat the sleek new furniture pieces that were upholstered in neutral shades, the room dividers and window coverings that unobtrusively directed light and movement within a given interior, the runners upon which sat the new ceramic vessels. And yet, suddenly, out of this monochrome world of thoughts and objects, emerged something totally different and essentially contradictory.

Having eliminated pattern and complicated weaves from the language of "contemporary" weaving, the "new" handweavers worked, as mentioned above, with a limited number of issues; texture and line became the conceptual vocabulary, a formalized language that was utilized in all of its possible permutations. These two physical realities, the line—created by the flexible element in warp and weft—and the sculptural possibilities of that same line-element whose manipulation could create textural reliefs, became the focus of weaving. The pioneer weavers of the '50s and '60s moved from the concerns of producing "good," anonymous designs to an exploration of what could be expressed by these formal properties themselves in focused isolation. And while that transition seemed very sudden, it resulted from the artists' conceptualization and visual consciousness as to the defining nature of their chosen medium, and the freedom of personal expression that was possible once the necessity of creating utilitarian "cloth" had been eliminated.

In the '60s, artists such as Lenore Tawney, Ed Rossbach, and Claire Zeisler investigated in depth the potential of the materials of textiles and the constructive possibilities for those pliable, linear elements. Fiber, and the ways in which it could be interlaced, became content.

In 1961 Lenore Tawney's works burst upon the scene, and the public was confronted by large, free-hanging pieces that moved away from walls, not only inhabiting human space, but dwarfing the human form by their monumental size. The woven plane was

Claire Zeisler's Preview, *1969; knotted and wrapped jute; 90 by 60 by 48 inches. Photo: courtesy the author.*

12

Ed Rossbach's Butterfly Basket, *1973; silkscreened, plaited paper; 10 by 12 by 9-1/2 inches. Photo: courtesy the artist; collection of Dr. and Mrs. Edward Okun, Santa Fe, New Mexico.*

slashed, opened, made transparent. One's eyes passed through the piece and recognized the space behind. Weaving was no longer fabric—a comfortable, predictable, understood commodity. And the loom ceased to determine the inevitable rectilinearity of form.

Experimentations with a variety of methods to achieve shaped weavings led weavers from the techniques of multilayered weaves and the shaping of the woven surface on the loom to manipulations of the woven plane after it had been woven. The process of weaving was no longer the end result, as completion was often predicated upon a series of activities that reworked the surface, fringe, and selvedge ends. Additive elements became common—feathers, beads, stitching, wrapping.

Once the woven surface became an arena for further activities, explorations intensified, not only in terms of experimenting with all possible materials, but also in terms of using other techniques that would free the maker from the restrictions imposed by the loom. Those explorations by individual artists were enhanced and encouraged by the publication of a number of influential books and the increasing accessibility of historic and ethnic examples of textiles from Third World countries. "Nonloom," a strangely imprecise term indicating a catchall category of diverse techniques, entered the textile lexicon.

The artist whose work most epitomized the experimental, rule-breaking mode of the '60s was Ed Rossbach. Broad in vision, accepting of spontaneous effects, problem-solving in methodology, Rossbach produced work that became a kind of sampler of textile possibilities. His great contribution to textiles resided in his ability, at that transitional moment in the late '50s/early '60s, to meld two very different positions. Contact with and study of historical textiles clearly indicated the expressive and iconic possibilities of fiber—they offered examples of techniques that were not tied to the mechanism of the loom, and they presented the possibility of textiles-as-object, a finite end-in-itself that need not seek completion by being part of something else. But to that new recognition he added the prevailing concerns of the "contemporary" designer-craftsman: experimentation with new materials, an emphasis on clearly stated structure, and the utilization of texture.

The period from the mid-'60s through the early '70s was a time of ferment and change, a period in which the term "counterculture" was coined in recognition that a single response to society no longer existed. During this period an immense range of textile possibilities opened up for artists, and their expressions were exuberant and ambitious. Textile activity was happening in two broad streams: one, emanating from the university- or art school-trained artist; the second, a populist movement of young people and adult females who were beginning to articulate their alienated or disenfranchised state from the larger culture.

The trained and professional artists were exploring the limits of their media; and the untrained were picking up techniques that were portable and free from exigencies of equipment and specialized space. One was creating formal, essentially abstract, and often medium-referential work; the other was creating coded-symbols, most often personal and intimate in size, that were visual expressions of their estranged state. The '60s gave us the simultaneous creation of a large, meditative Lenore Tawney and an anonymous, embroidered Levi jacket.

During the '70s, the shift among professional artists toward sculptural concerns was most fully expressed by Claire Zeisler's large, free-standing, knotted structures. No longer restricted to being a plane hanging in space, a textile had achieved volume, a full dimensionality that allowed the viewer to circumnavigate its form and view it from all perspectives. Zeisler's totemic forms encapsulated the dominant conceptual concerns of the medium at that particular moment, while also remarking on its ambivalent status. Her work was connected to an ancient past while attempting to negotiate an entrance into the contemporary world of Modernist art objects.

During the '70s, that ambivalency was the source of two dominant, parallel, and, again, contradictory developments that clearly were a continuance of the activities of the '60s. One was the creation of monumental works for public spaces; the other was the creation of small, intimate works having a visual, technical, or conceptual source in nonwestern tribal or ethnic textiles.

There was a recognition that the so-called "brutalist" architecture of the '70s could be softened and humanized by the addition of hanging woven reliefs. The term "woven walls" was used to both indicate current usage and to legitimize the form/usage by referring to its historic tapestry precursor, just as cement and steel skyscrapers became the contemporary equivalent of the stone castles of the Middle Ages.

This trend toward the monumental was encouraged and supported by the high-profile exhibitions happening biannually in Lausanne, Switzerland, and the influential examples of international work exhibited there. The overwhelming presence of a Magdalena Abakanowicz "Abakan" transformed the very notion of the comforting "niceness" of textiles. Rather than maintaining a western, subservient role, full of domestic connotations, textiles became a medium with which one could experience acute physical awareness and brooding expressionism.

In opposition to this monumentality, abstraction, and reductivist formality were intimate miniature textile works. Another group of artists, wanting to merge populist developments in art with the mystery and ritual importance of anthropological artifacts, began creating objects of small scale and intricate con-

Magdalena Abakanowicz at work on Yellow Abakan *(1967-68;
10 feet 3 inches by 10 feet 9 inches by 4 feet) and* Abakan Round
*(1967; 9 feet 10 inches by 3 feet 4 inches by 3 feet 4 inches); woven sisal.
Photo: © Jan Kosmowski, Warsaw, Poland, courtesy the artist.*

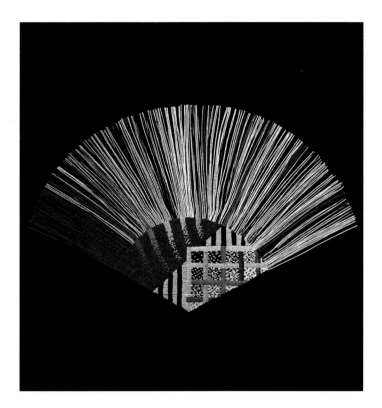

Top: Diane Itter's Fireworks Fan, 1980; *knotted linen; 10 by 16 inches.*
Photo: David Keister, courtesy William M. Itter.

Helena Hernmarck's Currency, 1992; *tabby, discontinuous tabby, freely picked soumak with linen warp, wool and linen weft; 9-1/2 by 28-1/2 feet. Photo: Brian Gassel; collection NationsBank, Atlanta, Georgia.*

struction. These works led to an increasingly narrative sense of personal storytelling. Shrines, altars, fetishes, and power garments were appropriated forms (and terms) that integrated the present with the past. They explored ancient values in contemporary terms and reiterated the traditional cultural importance of textiles to a world that had devalued them.

In the 1980s the proliferation of textile expression exploded into an amazing diversity of technical subsets: quilting, basketry, feltmaking, embroidery, printing, tapestry, sculptural forms, papermaking, computer-aided weaving, beading, performance, wearables, installations, sophisticated combinations of the above, and of textiles with other artforms ("mixed-media," "crossover art" became current designations) gave a broad profile to the field as well as a kind of fragmentation. The textile "ghetto" was often, in fact, a series of ghettoes rotating around certain individual teachers, organizations such as guilds, and specialized conferences. It became more difficult to single out dominant attitudes. A new "classicism" resided simultaneously with an archaeologically inspired primitivism. Complicated weave structures on computer-aided multiharness looms appeared alongside low-tech stitched cloth. The container form coexisted with space-transforming installations, and ritualistic performances with bland, corporate commissions.

But it was also a time of growing maturity both technically and conceptually. The textile arts field was coming into adulthood. Individual technical experimentation was largely unnecessary due to the reclaiming of information through publications, workshops, and learning institutions. Accessibility to current visual concerns and intellectual concepts had increased due to improved publications, including documentation in the form of catalogs of major exhibitions, and to national and international conferences and symposia. A self-conscious, unsure medium was becoming confident and assertive.

As financial support for public art and corporate collections had diminished (to the point of near invisibility!), the scale of work changed. The monumental had been replaced by work that was in a scale-relationship to the human body and whose projected home was now the space of human habitation. This worked, subliminally if not directly, to encourage the kind of storytelling that is implied by the human form, and a kind of intimacy required by the reduced space. Representation and narrative had returned; and stories were either being told directly or implied.

Artists of the '70s appropriated the forms of artifactual objects in their attempt to reconnect with the symbolic life that had surrounded the making and use of textiles since earliest times—a symbolic life rich in myth, metaphor, and allegory. But by the end of the '80s and into the early '90s, many artists had become uncomfortably aware that many of these anthropological objects functioned as material symbols of a ruling class, that as revered objects having symbolic and ritualistic meaning they had served to empower an elite social structure. Artists in the 1990s, having recaptured the historical importance of textiles, were now attempting to infuse that same sense of symbolic importance into the life of the common or "humble" textile: the textile created within the domestic sphere. The new "artifacts" used textiles, an outsider medium, to talk about the role of the outsider and tell the stories of the invisible peoples, those whose histories had been ignored and undervalued. The medium, again, in nonformal terms, became the message. And messages were being created not only through the use of visual icons and narrative structures, but much more overtly through the use of actual text as a companion to the visual.

With this topicality regarding current social issues and political positions becoming increasingly the subject of work done in the early 1990s, the subject matter of textiles becomes more difficult to extricate from the messages of work in other media. And the old issues of art versus craft begin to be superseded by questions of whether the future of textile arts should be one of integration with the mainstream art world or whether it should remain a separate entity or "a parallel universe." Questions of what could ultimately be lost or gained continue to be individually recognized and debated. In a postmodern age of appropriation, is the field itself being appropriated? And with what consequences?

Although this overview outlines some main trends in the development of visual expression and thought in the textile arts, it must be acknowledged (at least by this writer) that textiles is a medium without clear, self-defining boundaries or limitations. The energy in the field, from the 1960s on, has been generated by an attempt to discover the essential nature of textiles *and* by the concomitant realization that it illusively defies such definitions. Textiles has acted as a vacuum sucking up new materials, techniques, and modes of expression. It has changed its form, size, psychology, and philosophical stance. And those changes, continuing to occur, have not been linear, not ascending or descending, but exist simultaneously in amazingly diverse expressions. Fiber has adapted itself successfully to the concerns of the last four decades—just as it had previously done in the entire continuum of past human history.

Previous Page

JAN JANAS
UNITED STATES

A Question of Support

Acid dyed silk scraps floated in paper pulp, dried, and painted; 39 by 48-1/2 in.

The young woman supports the middle aged and older woman, but the circular movement is to show that each supports the other—emotionally, financially, and in every way.

A

MARJORIE MINK
UNITED STATES

Overlay: The Signs

Dyed, discharged, layered satin acetate and polyester; 24 by 28 in.

B

JULIA E. PFAFF
UNITED STATES

Triptych / Pottery in Another Context

Printing and fabric construction on hand dyed and painted cotton; 70 by 43-1/4 in. Photo: Taylor Dabney.

This piece is inspired by 13 years of working as an archaeological technical artist in Greece, Egypt, and Jordan. I see archaeology's quest for historical and cultural identity as a metaphor for the individual's search for identity.

C

LUCY A. JAHNS
UNITED STATES

Union

Dyeing, machine embroidery, and appliqué of cotton sailcloth and canvas; 53-1/2 by 36 in.

This was done as a wedding gift for my brother and his wife. I wanted it to be a piece that symbolized their commitment to each other—passionate in color and free in spirit.

A

B

C

D

D

JACQUES PETE
FRANCE

The Full-of-Dreams Suitcase
Batik on silk; 37 by 30 cm.

*My pictures are poems which mix
together dreams and daily life.*

E

CHRISTINE ZOLLER
UNITED STATES

Nocturnal Passage
Silkscreen and tape-resist
sponging of textile pigments on
canvas; 72 by 48 in. Photo:
David White.

E

A

**B E T S Y S T E R L I N G
B E N J A M I N**
JAPAN

Moon Eclipse

Roketsu-zome with *kinsai* on silk;
40 by 60 in. Photo: Ito.

B

D I A N A D A B I N E T T
CANADA

Flounder Rays

Serti resist and watercolor technique on silk twill; 143-1/2 by
128 cm.

*There are three species of flounder in
this piece. They can change their colors to blend in with their surroundings, but I have "captured" them here
in rays of sunlight.*

C

S ü Z E L B A C K
CANADA

The Theatre of the Annunciation

Wax resist, over-dyeing, and
shading on cotton sateen; 93 by
54 in. Photo: Daniel Roussel.

D

H Y U N - A H Y O O
KOREA

Life II

Wax resist dyeing on silk; 31 by
42 in.

*I am very happy and proud to be
making art using this traditional
technique.*

E

J E N I F E R A . B O R G
UNITED STATES

Window of the Guard

Silkscreen and direct application of textile pigment on canvas; 42 by 60 in. Photo: David
White.

*This piece was made partially as a
result of gingko leaves my daughter
gathered and presented to me.*

A

B

C

D

E

A

Lisa Clark
UNITED STATES

Espéranza - Hope

Image transfer, painting, and stitching using paper, fabric, and found objects; 23 by 27 by 1-1/2 in.

This explores the myriad of mixed messages that an individual receives from organized religion and various cultures. Curáme is Spanish for "heal me."

B

Delores Darby Smith
UNITED STATES

Angel Series

Cyanotype, silkscreen, and polychromatic dyeing on commercial fabric; 14 by 18 in.

C

Zia Sutherland
CANADA

e is for everything I

Stencil/discharge, silkscreen, beading, embroidery on cotton and silk organza; 11 by 12 in. Photo: Jim Henkel.

I am using the dress image to refer to uniform, costume, sophistication-turned-awkward, and women's subjugation.

A

B

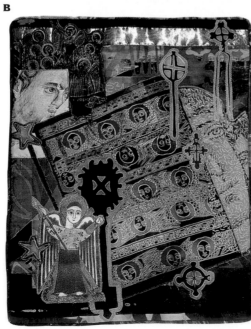

C

D

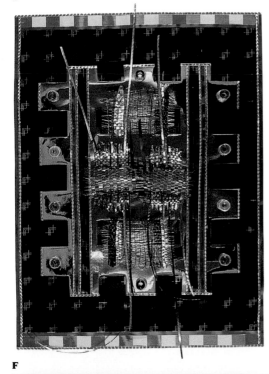

E

F

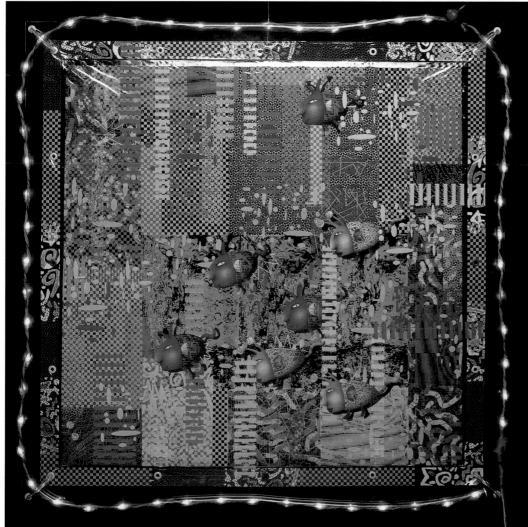

D

TRACY RUHLIN
UNITED STATES

Grid Miniature #10
Assemblage and plain weave
with hand-dyed monofilament,
copper wire, Mylar, decorative
sheeting, and plastic tubing;
9 by 12 in. Photo: Mary Helt.

I am continually intrigued by materi-
als connected to our high-tech society.

E

**FRAN GARDNER
PERRY**
UNITED STATES

Mystic Flight
Assemblage of found fabric,
painted paper, and beads;
15-1/2 by 20-1/2 by 2 in.
Photo: Fortune Photography.

F

YOSHIKO MATSUDA
UNITED STATES

Home Entertainment I
Sealed screen printed cotton
inside screen printed vinyl,
edged with rope light; 36 by 36
by 3/4 in

The focus of my work is to apply
creative, interactive elements to
entertain the viewer.

A

DONNA M. FLEMING
UNITED STATES

Carass I

Painting, drawing, piecing, embroidery, appliqué, and quilting on cotton; 39 by 42 in.

B

ILZE AVIKS
UNITED STATES

Complement Cloth

Discharge dyeing and seed stitch embroidery on cotton canvas; 55 by 55 in. Photo: Colorado State University Photo Services.

The relative limitation of the seed stitch precludes spontaneity in the usual sense, but the less personal mark imposes a strictness onto the cloth which, like a steady heartbeat, results in a combination of personal and anonymous expression.

C

ANNE MORRELL
ENGLAND

Rattlesnake

Dyed and embroidered even weave cotton; 57 by 46 cm. Photo: Stephen Yates.

I constantly watch and record the surface of my pond. I study the reflections, and I am inspired by the tension and harmony, boundary of air and water, edges.

D

KAY CAMPBELL
UNITED STATES

Nightdreams: Circling

Screen printing, stitching, and assemblage using silk and wood; 48 by 41 by 3 in. Photo: John Maul.

I have always been interested in observing and arranging objects in sequence, and in the patterns formed by repetitive motifs. In this piece, the resulting architectural reference of a window becomes a vantage point from which to view outer and inner emotions.

B

A

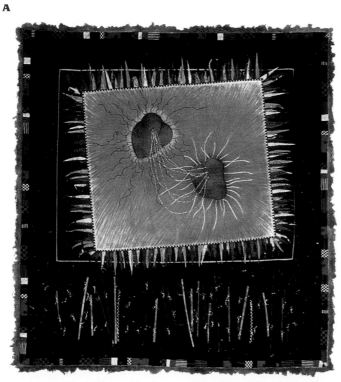

C

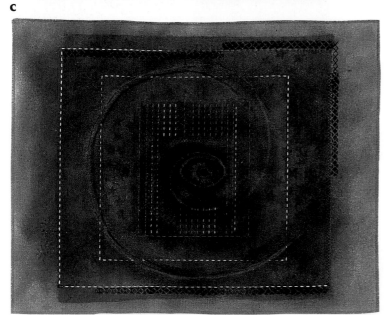

D

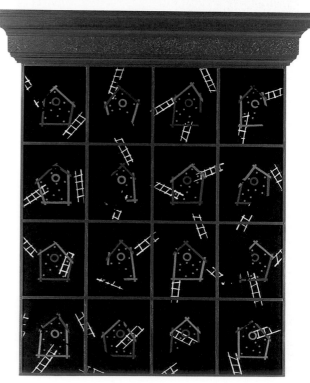

E

E

SONDRA L. DORN
UNITED STATES

My Chair

Photo silkscreen, painting, machine embroidery, and appliqué on canvas; 12 by 12 in. Photo: Walker Montgomery.

I have chosen to work in textiles because of our intimate but often unnoticed daily contact with them. The text refers to the kinds of communication we use in this culture and to the walls we can create with words.

F

CECILIA HJELM
SWEDEN

Zigzag

Dyeing, printing, and embroidery on cotton; 210 by 185 cm. Photo: Marlené Hamström.

F

A

AKEMI NAKANO COHN
UNITED STATES

Growth

Rice paste resist printing on silk; 56 by 43 in. Photo: Jay King.

There is a tension between the Eastern values with which I was raised and the Western values to which I am adjusting. I feel as if I have been "transplanted" to a new soil, and my work is an attempt to understand this experience.

B

MARTHA FERRIS
UNITED STATES

Somebody Called My Name

Silkscreen, stamping, wax resist printing, piecing, and embellishing on cotton, silk, and muslin; 82 by 65 by 2 in. Photo: Gretchen Haien.

The central images of the woman and the snake came to me in a powerful and disturbing dream; the title came after the piece was finished.

C

J ENNY C HIPPINDALE
ENGLAND

African Hanging

Dyeing, reverse appliqué, and couching on silk, cotton, and linen: 109 by 90 cm.

My source of inspiration for some time has been the woven, embroidered raffia cloth of Zaire.

D

L AURA F. C OHN
UNITED STATES

Ken Ken

Batik on cotton; 38 by 30 in. Photo: David Andrews.

E

**A STRID H ILGER
B ENNETT**
UNITED STATES

Passage

Resist dyeing and hand painting on hand woven cotton; 23 by 23 in.

Pattern fascinates me. In nature, overlays of pattern occur universally, and my images often refer to natural phenomena.

F

A NN S MITH
ENGLAND

Ndebele People

Batik and machine stitching on calico; 90 by 90 cm.

C

D

E

F

D

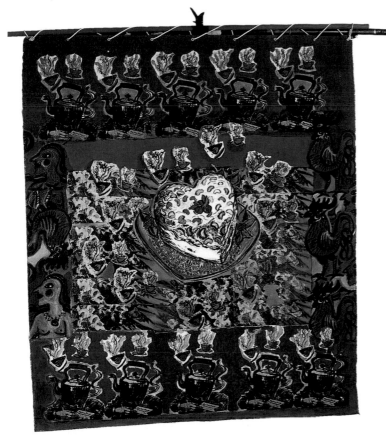

E

A

GREG SOMERVILLE
AUSTRALIA

Happiness, Silence, Nothing

Screen printing, Seminole patchwork, appliqué, and quilting on cotton; 380 by 150 cm.

In this piece, I am dealing with fractal scaling, natural rhythms, and human perception of pattern.

B

MARY TYLER
UNITED STATES

Night River #1

Hot wax batik on pieced and quilted cotton; 40 by 48 in. Photo: Zolton Cohen.

C

ROBERTA GLIDDEN
UNITED STATES

Leaves

Hot wax resist brush-applied dyeing on silk; 24 by 36 in.

D

LYNNE LOMOFSKY
CANADA

Tea, Cake & Flowers

Silkscreen printing and hand painting on canvas; 60 by 70 in. Photo: Lorena Barrera.

The textiles of Africa, with their lively visual imagery, vibrant colors, and bold patterning are the inspiration for my work.

E

TRICIA COULSON
UNITED STATES

Seeing Through the Obsession

Silkscreened, pieced, and machine stitched silk organza; 59 by 69 by 4 in. Photo: Lee Bale.

The investment of an incredible amount of time, so out of sync with today's production-oriented values, produces a rhythm which soothes me into timelessness.

A

NOEL DYRENFORTH
ENGLAND

Spring

Batik on cotton; 125 by 95 cm.

B

LOUISA SIMONS
ENGLAND

Fiesta II

Painting and collage on silk; 60 by 60 cm.

C

MARIE-LAURE ILIE
UNITED STATES

Emergence

Hand painting with dyes on silk and organza; 53 by 54 by 1 in.

D

M. JOAN LINTAULT
UNITED STATES

The Flower Thieves

Hand dyed, painted, screen printed, pieced, and quilted cotton; 82 by 93 in. Photo: Daniel Overturf.

I am illustrating the delicate balance between creation and destruction.

E

EDWARD S. LAMBERT
UNITED STATES

Convoluted Camouflage

Screen print, monoprint, and direct painting on canvas; 95 by 54-1/2 in.

This deals with the conflicts between man and nature—man's pollution of the earth vs. nature's attempt to rectify the assaults on it.

A

B

C

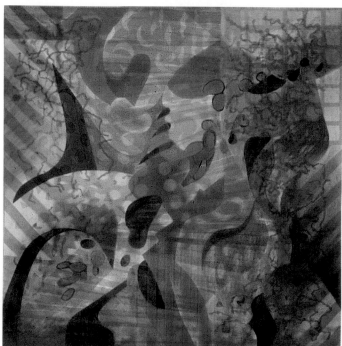

E

31

A

HYANG SOOK PARK
KOREA

Hometown

Silkscreen and wax painting on silk; 120 by 200 cm. Photo: Man-Hong Lee.

B

CLARE VERSTEGEN
UNITED STATES

Angles © 1993

Screen printed and painted cotton; 56 by 90 in.

C

BARBARA J. MORTENSON
UNITED STATES

Sins of the Fathers

Dye transfer, photo copy, machine embroidery, and appliqué on satin, silk, and cotton; 58 by 48 in. Photo: Gary McKinnis.

At the same time that a Klan rally was to take place in my township, I found an old image of two KKK men and a baby dressed in hoods. We do pass a heritage on to our children, whatever it is.

D

MARCIA KARLIN
UNITED STATES

Masquerade II

Cyanotype and inkodye printed, painted, machine pieced, appliquéd, and quilted cotton and sheers; 33 by 41-1/2 in.

In response to advertising copy and other social messages, we construct masks that conceal and imprison us from these messages.

E

KATHY WEAVER
UNITED STATES

Guns Are Us, Funerary Piece One

Silkscreening, painting, appliqué, and quilting on cotton and satin; 78 by 82 in. Photo: Nelson Armour.

After teaching in two Chicago schools serving housing projects, and now teaching on the North Shore, I learned there are undue weights on some children. Those in the ghetto do not seem to count as much. My experiences, many conversations I've had, and the Chicago Tribune's tally of children killed in 1992 were used as source material for this piece.

A

B

C

D

E

A

JUDITH MCNALLY-WARNER
UNITED STATES

Equivoquilt

Monotype, Xerox transfer, computer graphics, pieced, and quilted cotton; 60 by 60 in. Photo: Courtney Frisse.

This is a humorous look at my serious aesthetic contemplations.

B

SHIRLEY HOW
UNITED STATES

Wallpiece Kimono

Acrylic paint on organza; 75 by 57 in. Photo: Suzanne Lacke.

As an Asian, I am basically influenced and inspired by Eastern art.

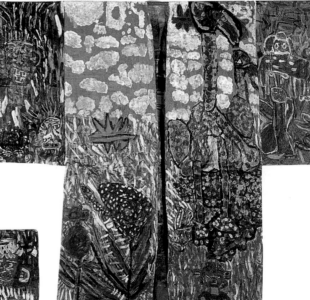

C

D

C

HEATHER CONNELLY
ENGLAND

La Table Devant La Fenêtre

Screen printing, stenciling, and painting on silk; 88 by 277 cm. Photo: Keith Tidball.

This work was inspired by a trip to Paris, and is part of a series in which I am attempting to evoke the atmosphere and romantic nature of the city.

D

MARTHA DESPOSITO
UNITED STATES

Monumental Cat

Painting, drawing, and collage on canvas; 32 by 73 in.

My paternal and maternal grandmothers were continually sewing, quilting, hooking rugs, making dolls and costumes, so I was surrounded by textiles. My need to paint has naturally evolved to its present form of combining the two media.

E

KAY HENNING DANLEY
UNITED STATES

Koi

Dye applied with sponges and brushes, metallic paint on silk; 64-3/8 by 34-1/2 in. Photo: Bill Bachhuber.

E

KAREN L. MCCARTHY
UNITED STATES

Flight of Fancy

Pigmented starch paste, drawing, and stitching on papers using oil and chalk pastels and colored pencil; 30 by 30 in.

I manipulate pigmented starch paste with everything from combs to cookie cutters to get the patterns I want; next, I work into the surface with colored pencil and stitchery. Paste papers have traditionally been used as book endpapers, and I am seeking to expand their expressive potential.

B

LINDA LEVIN
UNITED STATES

Composition III

Dyed, machine pieced and quilted cotton; 30 by 40 in. Photo: Image Inn.

A

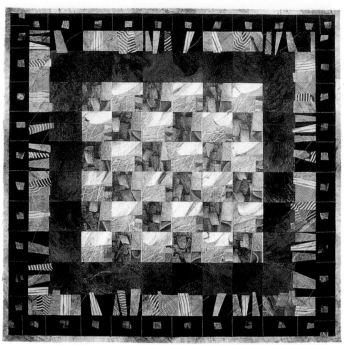

C

B

36

D

E

A

TONY DYER
AUSTRALIA

Deep Impressions

Batik, appliqué, and machine stitching on silk and canvas; 62 by 46 in.

B

SANDRA L. WILES
CANADA

The Lady of Shalott

Painting, appliqué, and machine stitching on cotton and canvas; 84 by 72 in.

The reference to, and the use of, textiles recalls the oppressed history of women, yet champions their quietly powerful "crafts."

A

B

C

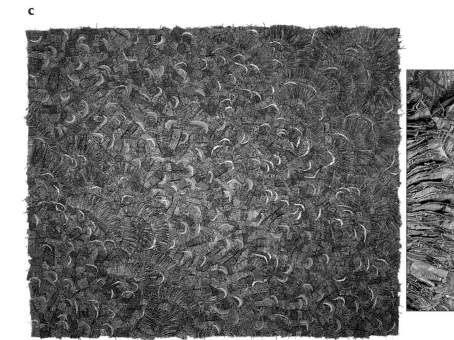

D

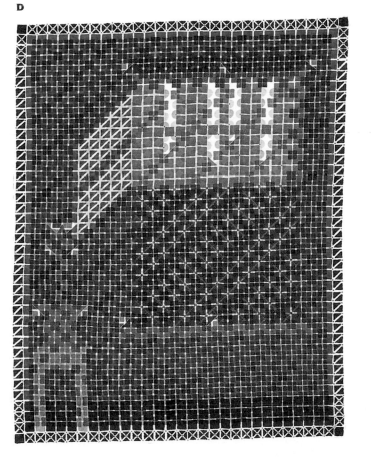

C

SUSAN WILCHINS
UNITED STATES

Sea Mantle: Acmaeidae

Dyed, screen printed, pieced, appliquéd, and stitched cotton and synthetic metallic fabrics; 54 by 45 by 1 in. Photo: Marc Wilchins.

I find working with fabric as natural as breathing, and its expressions a "language" that is often more eloquent than English itself.

D

JEANNE WILLIAMSON
UNITED STATES

Icicles

Hand stamped and machine quilted cotton; 36-1/2 by 46-1/4 in. Photo: David Caras.

I have a lot of patience. There are over 2500 stamped shapes in this piece!

E

ELIZABETH WADSWORTH- MANDELL
UNITED STATES

And So Much More

Dyed, pieced, and tied cotton; 49 by 57 in.

E

A

BETTE USCOTT-WOOLSEY
UNITED STATES

Expedition #1

Painting and embroidery on silk; 25-1/2 by 21-1/4 in. Photo: Will Brown.

B

SANDRA SIDER
UNITED STATES

Women at Work and Play, no. 1

Color xerography, stenciling, embroidery, and machine piecing and quilting on cotton; 38 by 54 in. Photos transferred to fabric by Aneta Sperber of photoTextiles.

This is a portrait study of photographer Kristen Olson Murtaugh.

C

PAMELA BECKER
UNITED STATES

Tulipa

Painting, stamping, piecing, and appliqué on cotton/polyester; 30 by 37 by 5 in.

Using the landscape both as a source of ideas and of color, I construct images which reflect my concern with the "ideal" in nature.

D

CAROL ADLEMAN
UNITED STATES

The Pear

Cyanotype printing, painting with dyes, piecing, and quilting on cotton; 38 by 33-1/2 in. Photo: Michael Keefe.

Cyanotype on fabric has been my focus since 1981, and it is still fascinating and challenging. In this piece, the fabric was "scrunched" during printing, thus the shadows were printed onto the painted surface.

E

DOMINIE NASH
UNITED STATES

Peculiar Poetry 4

Dyeing, screen printing, drawing, machine appliqué and quilting on cotton and silk; 43 by 43 in. Photo: Mark Gulezian.

The garden, seen in different light and weather, is the guiding imagery for this piece.

A

B

D

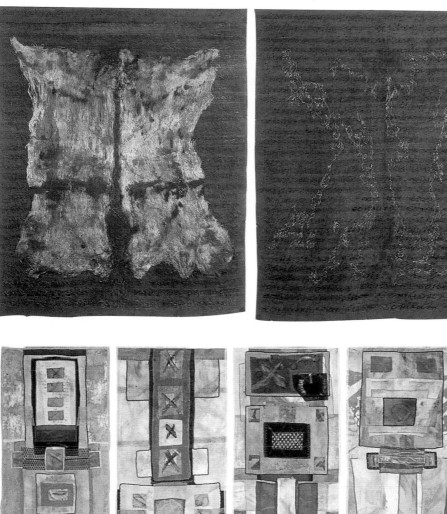

E

EMILY RICHARDSON
UNITED STATES

Then We Were Six

Painting, staining, drawing, appliqué, embroidery, and couching on silk, cotton, linen, and miscellaneous fabrics; 107 by 73 in. Photo: Gary McKinnes.

The similar motifs in the six panels represent the common qualities found within a family; the uniqueness of each panel represents the growth and changes which family members confront.

E

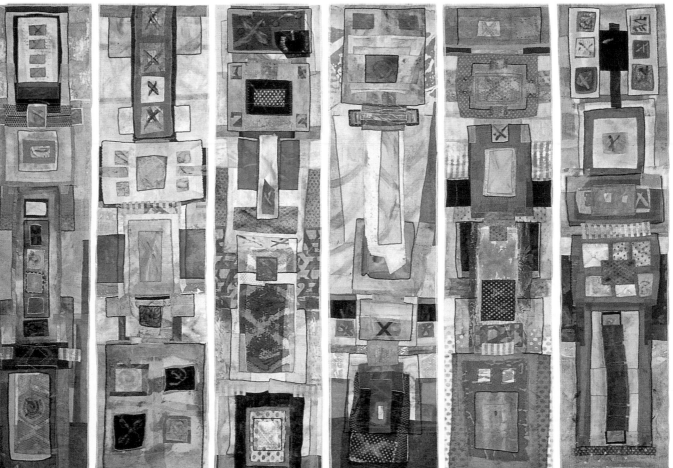

D

E

F

A

CHERRY PARTEE
UNITED STATES

Memory and Hope

Batik, stamping, piecing, embroidery, and quilting on cotton; 76 by 95 in. Photo: Grover Partee.

B

CHRIS ALLEN-WICKLER
UNITED STATES

Leaf Resist (details)

Picked leaves pinned to living vine leaves, which were left over a period of five weeks so that patterns formed; full piece 96 by 96 in.

This low-tech stenciling reminds me of photosynthesis which is, after all, a primal form of photography.

C

CATHERINE LA DU
UNITED STATES

The Great Divide

Photo copy transfer, stamping, piecing, machine stitching, appliqué, and quilting on commercial fabrics; 67 by 51 in. Photo: Precision Photographics.

I like to play and make puns with words, ideas, and materials. The techniques of photo copy transfer and fabric collage allow me to indulge in this pleasure.

D

ERMA MARTIN YOST
UNITED STATES

Forest Elegy

Cyanotype, embroidery, and machine quilting on cotton and synthetic fabric; 28 by 26 by 3 in. Photo: courtesy Noho Gallery, New York City.

Forests are precious eco-systems that are being clearcut and mismanaged to the brink of extinction. The viewer is invited to ponder pristine landscapes that soon may not be there.

E

LINDA R. MACDONALD
UNITED STATES

Spotted Owl vs. Chain Saw: Wild & Tasty

Dyed, airbrushed, painted, and stitched cotton; 51 by 65 in. Photo: Amy Frenzel.

In northern California where I live, the political atmosphere is thick with polarities: environmentalists and loggers; jobs and unemployment, BMWs and pickup trucks.

F

NANILEE S. ROBARGE
UNITED STATES

Autumn Joy

Screen printing, painted warp, and weaving using cotton; 68 by 68-1/4 in.

528

L E E B A L E
UNITED STATES

Magic Carpet Ride

Screen and stencil printing on
nylon net; 60 by 96 by 34 in.

*The decision to position myself as an
artist working with cloth and domestic
textile production can be viewed as a
political stance.*

864

J A C Q U E L I N E
T R E L O A R
CANADA

Guardians For Jamie

Painting, heat transfer,
appliqué, and beading on
transluscent polyester; 90 by 96
in. each panel.

A

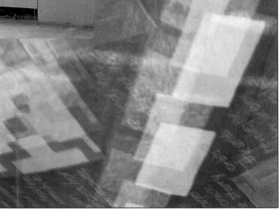

B

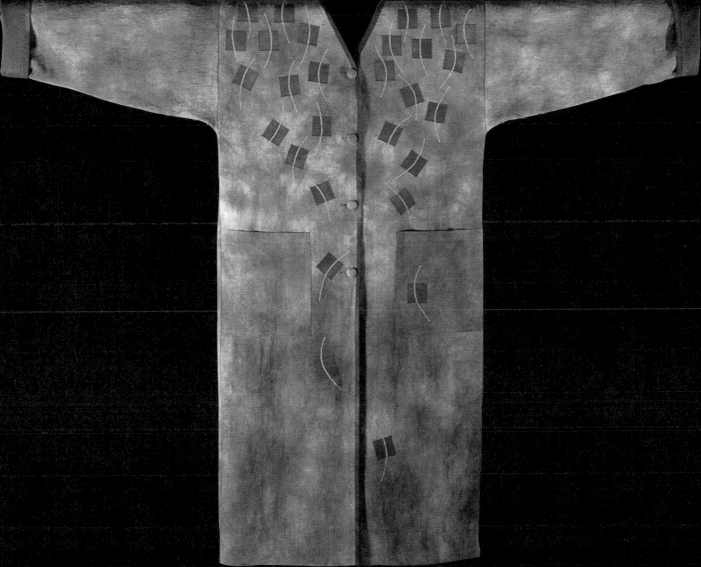

Previous Page

ANNA CARLSON
UNITED STATES

Untitled Duster

Hand dyed and over dyed linen with appliqué and embroidery. Photo: Wayne Torborg.

Using the shibori bundle-and-dye technique, various materials are dyed, rinsed, and dyed again. The garment designs are simple and classic in order to accent the fabric and embellishment.

A

JOANNE WOLL
UNITED STATES

Kimono Series / Star Flower

Shibori with fiber reactive dyes on cotton. Photo: Red Elf, Inc., St. Louis, Missouri.

B

CHERIE ST. CYR
UNITED STATES

Shibori Jacket

Shibori and wax resist over-painting on silk crepe de chine. Photo: Dennis Church.

This piece was made while I was an artist-in-residence in Nepal. After finishing it, I left it overnight...not realizing that condensation drips off the ceiling. Before tearing my hair out the next morning, I managed to save the jacket by re-salting and drying it out.

C

MAUDE DIGGS
UNITED STATES

Geometric Pleated Coat

Hand woven, ikat dyed, discharge printed, and hand painted cotton and silk. Photo: Monico Candelaria.

My mother, Jo Diggs, is a fiber artist. Growing up in her studio, I learned to sew, to love fabric and color, and to cherish creative solitude.

A

B

C

D

TRACY MARTIN
UNITED STATES

Freedom of the Press

Arashi shibori and hand paint-ing on silk, embellished with glass seed and bugle beads, buttons of polymer clay. Photo: John S. Payne.

This is a celebration of a fundamental right that should not be controlled or diminished.

E

GINA D'AMBROSIO
UNITED STATES

Spirit Windows

Warp painting, hand weaving, shibori, overpainting and print-ing on silk. Photo: Monico Candelaria.

I am fascinated by windows—revealing, opening, closing, and letting us "frame" in what we see, often forming grids so that what we see seems like a mosaic.

E

A

JANE KENYON
CANADA

Autumn Splendor

Painted warp, dyed weft, hand woven silk. Photo: Grant Kernan.

As a painter and a fiber artist, warp painting has fulfilled my need to paint while allowing me to pursue my love of weaving.

B

ANNE GLUM
GERMANY

Dragon Rocks

Watercolor and gutta resist painting on silk satin.

A

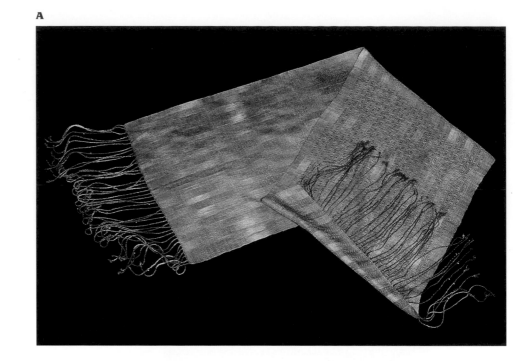

B

C

DORLE STERN-STRAETER
GERMANY

Twenty Kimonos - Plenty Kimonos

Crazy patchwork, machine sewing, hand quilting of old Japanese kimono silk. Photo: Patricia Fliegauf.

In 1992, I had an exhibition and gave lectures and workshops in Japan. This kimono is in memory of that time.

D

CHUNGHIE LEE
KOREA

Black Soul

Hand dyeing, slashing, layering, and machine stitching of cotton.

Contemporary dancer Lee Jung Hee is wearing the dress. Her dance was for those who died during the harsh days of the past.

E

WENDY RICHARDSON
UNITED STATES

Night Brites

Piecing, printing, and layering of cotton and raw silk.

D

E

A

ULRIC PAUL PEREIRA
CANADA

Untitled Ties

Screen printed and hand painted silk.

In a fusion of past and present, the 17th-century celestial map reproductions take on a modern edge in the form of functional wearable art.

B

LINDA FRANCE HARTGE AND DAVID HARTGE
UNITED STATES

Orchid Scarf

Gutta resist painted silk crepe de chine. Photo: David Hartge.

C

RITA LENN
UNITED STATES

Fish Coat

Gutta resist-painted with French dyes on silk.

A

B

C

D

E

F

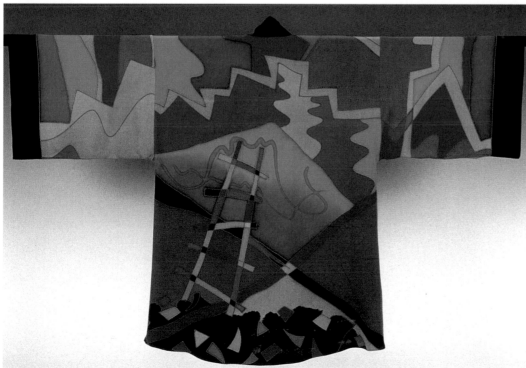

D

ROSITA PARDO
UNITED STATES

Sumo Wrestler Scarves

Resist-painted silk. Photo: Suzanne Lacke.

E

PEGGOTTY CHRISTENSEN
UNITED STATES

Jacket

Brush painted silk using fiber reactive dyes. Photo: Bruce Talbot.

The design elements are my interpretation of motifs found on Native American pottery and rugs.

F

KIM HUBER
UNITED STATES

Aztec Skyscape

Resist painted silk crepe de chine. Photo: Jerry Anthony.

A

LENE NIELSEN
DENMARK

Cobweb Felted Scarves (detail)

Tussah silk and merino wool.

My philosophy entails a dear respect for craftsmanship which, to me, incorporates knowledge, skill, and technique.

B

BARBARA KLAER AND JUDITH KLAER-KERNS
UNITED STATES

Poppy Coat

Hand painted with fiber reactive dyes on silk. Photo: George Anderson.

This is our acceptance of Georgia O'Keeffe's invitation to "travel inside the poppy petals."

C

JOY STOCKSDALE
UNITED STATES

Golden Net

Polychromatic screen printing on silk. Photo: Kate Cameron.

The technique, which I developed, is a combination of painting and printing with dyes.

A

B

C

D

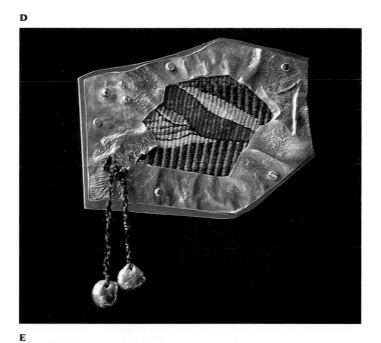

E

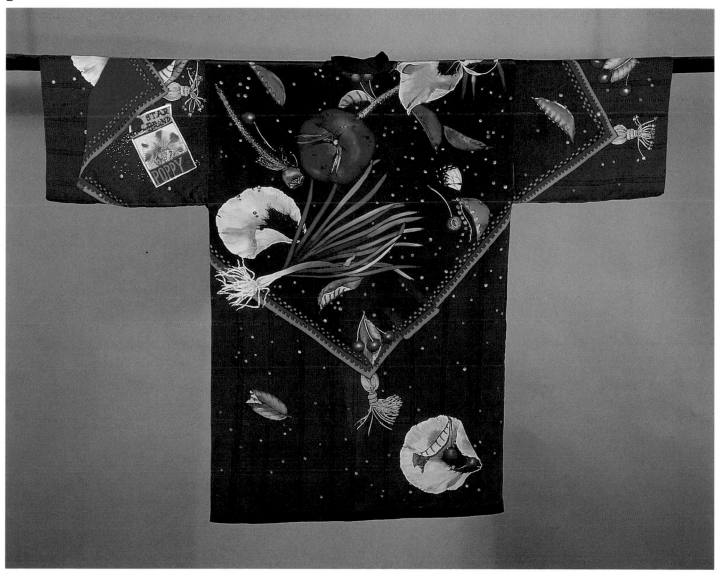

D

GAIL GAGNON-GARCIA
UNITED STATES

Molten Brooch

Cotton tapestry and sterling silver. Photo: Terry Davitt-Powell.

My pieces are done to achieve the best solution from a weaving point of view, but I especially love the combination of the sheen of the silver and the texture of the tapestry.

E

LINDA FRANCE HARTGE AND DAVID HARTGE
UNITED STATES

Black Table Cloth Kimono

Gutta resist painted silk crepe de chine. Photo: David Hartge.

To create the effect of a scarf wrapped around the shoulders, we painted in tassels and the flipped-up corner

A

HEATHER MARTIN
ENGLAND

Oystershell Jacket

Block printed, hand painted and quilted dyed cotton. Photo: David Harding.

B

SARA L. SCOTT
UNITED STATES

Ripples of Gold

Quilted and slashed silk.

C

BIRD ROSS
UNITED STATES

Reversible Jacket

Machine pieced and stitched rayon and cotton.

I swore I wouldn't make wearables to try to sell because of the issues of "size, sex, and season" (who wears it when, and how big or small are they?). But...I couldn't resist! So now I make them in one adaptable size, for either gender, out of fabrics that excite me.

D

JOANELL CONNOLLY
UNITED STATES

Body Quilt

Dyeing, direct painting, machine piecing and quilting of silk and silk/cotton blend. Photo: Portraits On Location; model Erin Connolly.

My intent was to create an elegant garment that had the feel of a really comfortable quilt.

A

B

C

D

E

F

E

CAROLYN DAHL AND LISA SHARP
UNITED STATES

Blue Norther Coat

Hand-dyed and quilted cotton corduroy and velvet, embellished with beads and metallic thread, lined with hand-dyed silk.

F

KAREN JAMES SWING
UNITED STATES

Perennial English Garden

Machine pieced, appliquéd, and quilted cotton. Photo: Michael Siede.

A

LESLIE CHRISTINE GELBER
UNITED STATES

Pink Pinatas

Machine appliqué and hand beading on denim, cotton, and lamé. Photo: Dave McKay, Photography Unlimited.

B

SHARMINI WIRASEKARA
CANADA

Heaven and Hell Reversible Coat

Cold wax resist painted silk crepe de chine. Photo: Barbara Cohen.

My objective is to create a greater aware-ness and recognition of wearable art.

C

JUDITH PINNELL
AUSTRALIA

Camelot

Beading, machine embroidery, painting, and stitching.

This is me in a romantic mood. Just because I'm a grandmother, it doesn't mean I can't feel romantic.

D

NANC MEINHARDT
UNITED STATES

Evening Bag

Off loom-woven glass seed beads, silk cord, ultra suede. Photo: Tom Vaneynde.

E

NATACHA WOLTERS
GERMANY

Geometrical Necklace

Crocheting with lapis lazuli, seed and glass beads. Photo: C. Wolters.

F

CAROL WILCOX WELLS
UNITED STATES

Flower of Aphrodite

Hand woven glass seed beads using the peyote stitch. Photo: Tim Barnwell.

Textiles, nature, and medieval illumi-nations are the inspiration for my choices of patterns, colors, and shapes.

A

B

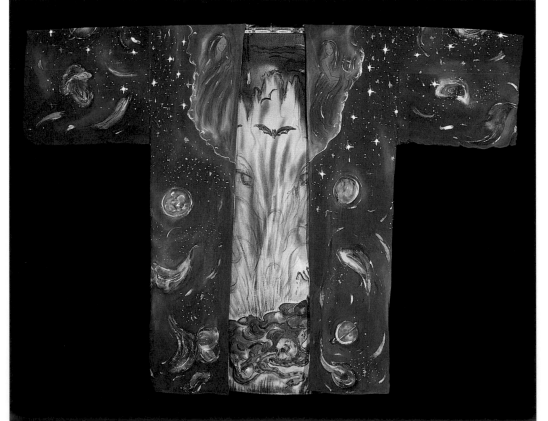

C

D

E

F

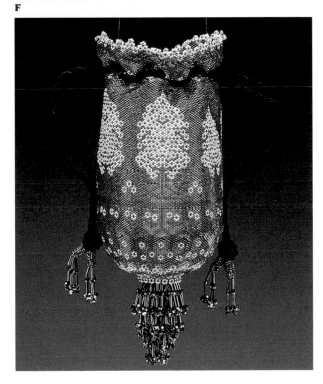

A

BARBARA BRANDEL
UNITED STATES

Hunting Jacket

Hand woven tapestry weave of cotton, silk, and wool. Photo: Mary Findysz.

Modern hunter/gatherers can wear this visual comment on the primitive practice of weaving dead animal skins.

B

CHARLOTTE TORGOVITSKY
UNITED STATES

Linda's Feathers

Machine appliqué, hand lacing, handcut fringing of deerskin. Photo: George Post.

The hand lacing technique I use is borrowed from the decorative saddlery stitching of the Old West.

C

LINDA K. SAGE
UNITED STATES

2-4-T (Two for Tea)

Double-bed machine knitting of 5/2 pearl cotton using an original hand-punched pattern card. Photo: Richard Schaffner; painting by Ed Tomlinson.

A stylish tea enjoyed with my sister in York, England was the inspiration for this coat; I then gave it to my sister/ author Rosemary Sage for her birthday.

D

LINDA WELKER
UNITED STATES

Winter Sky Dance / Sky Series

Hand knitted kid mohair, handspun boucle, lambswool, sterling silver buttons by Mark Oberzil. Photo: David Browne.

The series is a direct extension of my paintings and collages, grounded in a landscape tradition that seeks to evoke a particular season, time of day, or quality of light. Spinning the boucle for a jacket like this takes nearly 200 hours.

E

GABRIELLE RENSCH
CANADA

Repose

Hand knitted kid mohair, mohair, acrylic, wool, nylon, and cotton. Photo: Lionel Stevenson, Camera Art.

A

B

F

RUTH E. LANTZ
UNITED STATES

Intergalactic Cocoon

Computer generated graphics with double-bed Jacquard knitting using cotton. Photo: George C. Anderson.

The garments I've been making for more than 16 years are designed so that the fabric is the focus. I keep the styling simple so that the garments can be worn from year to year and will never be "out" of style.

A

STELA GAZZANEO
BRAZIL

Kadiweu II

Weaving with wool. Photo:
Irene Santos.

*Even though I've always been inter-
ested in the textile arts, I didn't take
up working in them until I retired in
1989. This piece is inspired by the
body makeup and decorative paintings of Brazilian Indians.*

B

LORRAINE JACKSON AND PAUL FRIEDMAN
UNITED STATES

Untitled Coat

Seminole patchwork and
piecing of cotton and rayon
Jacquard, glass beading. Photo:
Bill Murphy.

*We have been working together since
1979. Our greatest rewards come
from creating pieces for specific clients.*

C

ED JOHNETTA MILLER
UNITED STATES

Many Cultures Collide

Machine pieced fabrics from
Mali, Ghana, Guatemala,
Panama, Peru, Senegal, and the
United States.

A

B

C

D

JUNANNE PECK
UNITED STATES

African Mask Coat / Dreamstealer Cape

Canvas painted with fabric dye.
Photo: Natalie Caudill

In 1989, I started taking the images from my paintings and putting them on clothing I market under the name, "Body Canvases."

E

SANDY WEBSTER
UNITED STATES

African Canvas

Stitching and embellishing of mudcloth and other fabrics.

This was inspired by the women of West Africa and the Margaret Courtney-Clarke book, African Canvas.

F

JACKIE PETERS CULLY
UNITED STATES

Antelope

Direct wax technique of applying dye on silk.

This is inspired by the African antelope sculptures of Mali.

E

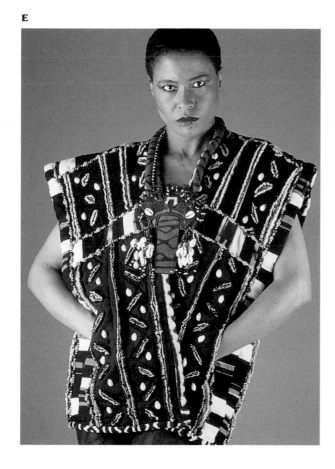

F

A

KATHLEEN M. RICHERT
UNITED STATES

Party Dress

Piecing and sewing of snackfood packages (fully lined).

I especially like this dress because it stands by itself.

B

JAN HAMILTON
ENGLAND

Quell

Hand dyed, machine knitted, pieced and patched wool and cashmere. Photo: Jay Whitcombe.

C

ROSE KELLY
UNITED STATES

Flak Jacket

Resist-painted and -dyed silk.

This jacket will protect me from urban and natural danger—theft, snarling dogs, earthquakes, and electromagnetic fields.

A

B

C

D

CAROL McKIE MANNING
UNITED STATES

Tree of Life

Appliqué, quilting, embroidery, beading, painting and stamping on silk, rayon, and polyester. Photo: Tom Henderson.

E

ELLEN J. HUTCHINSON
UNITED STATES

Peacock Coat

Hand and machine sewing and painting on silk. Photo: Brad Miller.

A

SUSAN HOLMES
NEW ZEALAND

Rainbow Warrior

Stencil printing, hand dyeing, and appliqué on crinkled silk, velvet, and spinnaker cloth. Photo: Phil Fogle.

The Greenpeace ship sunk in Auckland by the French was called Rainbow Warrior. Mine goes to war using the womanly qualities of lightness and beauty, defending truth with radiance and directness.

B

MARY RUSSELL
UNITED STATES

Even Cowgirls Get the Blues

Patchwork and appliqué using cotton, ultrasuede, and silk.

This is the ultimate fantasy for me. I grew up on a ranch and still work as one of the hired hands. As a child, I often played "cowboys and Indians," but I was never this well dressed.

B

C

D

E

C

MARGARET ROACH
WHEELER
UNITED STATES

Requiem of the Raven

Construction with summer/winter handwoven silk/wool. Photo: courtesy *Shuttle, Spindle & Dyepot.*

My direction, which included painting and metal sculpting, changed dramatically when I was required to teach weaving. Although I grew up in a household where fiber was a part of daily life, I did not consider it to be integral to my artistic work. Now I feel that my training, heritage, and artistic ability have found completion in the act of weaving.

D

NICK CAVE
UNITED STATES

Sound Suit - Garment

Mixed media with cotton, afghan, beads, metal, and wood. Photo: Stephen Hamilton.

E

GWYNN POPOVAC
UNITED STATES

Kitamura

Plaster gauze casting covered with rice paper, cotton rag paper painted and etched with pencil, woven beads, braiding. Photo: Michael Denny.

This was designed for the Sierra Repertory Theatre's production of Philip Kan Gotanda's Kabuki-style play, "The Dream of Kitamura." The character is a spirit monster symbolizing anything humans fear, especially themselves.

A

SUE BROAD
NEW ZEALAND

Cocoon Wrap

Hand woven, warp painted and hand dyed tussah silk. Photo: Brendan Lodge.

B

PAMELA WHITLOCK
UNITED STATES

Baseball Caps

8-harness shadow weave using silk, viscose, and rayon chenille, lined with washed rayon. Photo: Gary Warnimont.

C

GISELLE SHEPATIN
UNITED STATES

Untitled

Woven chenille and polyester top; cotton, silk, and suede skirt; necklace by Susan Green. Photo: Tia Dodge.

D

KIM YOST MERCK
UNITED STATES

Textured Rainbow Scarves: Geometric Series

Computer-generated patterns, dip-dyed warp, hand woven cotton and silk. Photo: John Toth.

E

ALLISON DENNIS
UNITED STATES

Double Alchemy Reversible Jacket

Hand woven cotton with a computer-aided design. Photo: Sheila Goode.

A

B

C

D

E

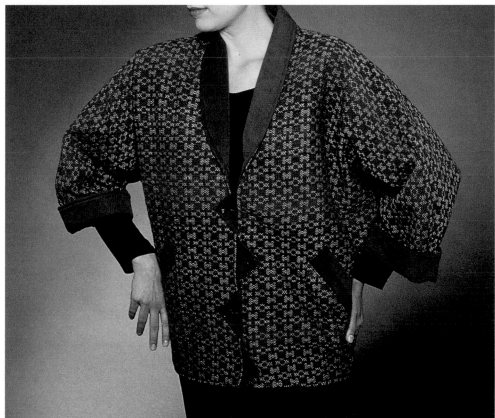

A

ANN RICHARDS
ENGLAND

Square Waves (detail)

Hand dyed and hand woven silk and wool.

The fabric remains flat while it is on the loom and the texture develops in the finishing. High twist wool, in the lower layer of the cloth, shrinks when the piece is washed, throwing the upper layer of silk into relief.

B

MOLLIE FREEMAN
UNITED STATES

Handwoven Warp-Painted Jacket

Plain weave, mixed warp of cottons/rayons with a wool weft. Photo: David McKay.

C

PIA FILLIGER-NOLTE
GERMANY

Plangi-Plissee

Hand woven and tie-dyed cashmere/silk.

A

C

B

NEEDLEWORK
· · · · · · ·

Previous Page

NanC Meinhardt
UNITED STATES

Miss Stitch

Bead embroidery with glass and metal seed beads, French knots, sewing and piecing of fabric; 19-1/2 by 20 by 2-1/2 in. Photo: Jerry Kobylecky.

Beads seem to chant. Each bead is a tiny vessel of visual tone and, when bound together with other beads, forms a chorus of light and tone that creates sumptuous surfaces.

A

Collis Caroline Marshall
UNITED STATES

Through the Looking Glass

Loom-woven glass beads, cotton and nylon warp threads, cotton batting on linen; 6-1/2 by 6-1/2 in. Photo: Geoffrey Carr.

The empty glass the rabbit offers is a reminder to myself not to dwell on the past.

B

Anne Kincaid
UNITED STATES

Dancing to Jerusalem

Collage appliqué transferred to fabric then embroidered and beaded; 14 by 10 in. Photo: Mark Frey.

Working with Jungian archetypes, I reach toward creating contemporary icons based on sacred personal imagery.

C

Connie Lehman
UNITED STATES

Santa Sofia of Leaves

Russian needlepunch and embroidery using glass beads and sequins; 8-1/2 by 3-5/8 in.

D

CAROL BURNS
UNITED STATES

La Esperanza

Beads and sequins hand stitched onto fabric; 28 by 24 inches.

I have always marveled at the way Haitian artists use thousands of delicate stitches, sequins, and beads to produce such bold, powerful, and expressive images. Their techniques and the religious artwork of the Hispanic peoples of the southwestern United States were the inspiration for this piece.

E

SANDRA GAYLE NICKESON
UNITED STATES

Emergency Visionectomy © 1992

Stitching, drawing, and beading using cotton, foil wrapped, and silk threads; 13-1/4 by 11-3/4 in. Photo: Red Elf.

This is about divorce—mine—and strikes me paradoxically as very funny and very sad.

F

LINDA LEWIS
UNITED STATES

War

Glass beads embroidered onto canvas; 17 by 16-3/4 in.

The Gulf War was the impetus for this piece.

A

B

A

JULIANNA MAHLEY
UNITED STATES

Prunella: Wearing the Artist's Hat

Surface stitchery and beading on painted fabric; 8 by 7 in.

B

KARIN BIRCH
UNITED STATES

The New Madonna

Embroidery, peyote stitch beadwork, and painted matte board; 9 by 12 in. Photo: Harriet Wise.

C

JOAN WOLFER
UNITED STATES

Looking On

Embroidery, beading, and painting on evenweave canvas; 36 by 40 in. Photo: Amaranth. Collection of Schacht Spindle Company, Inc., Boulder, Colorado.

C

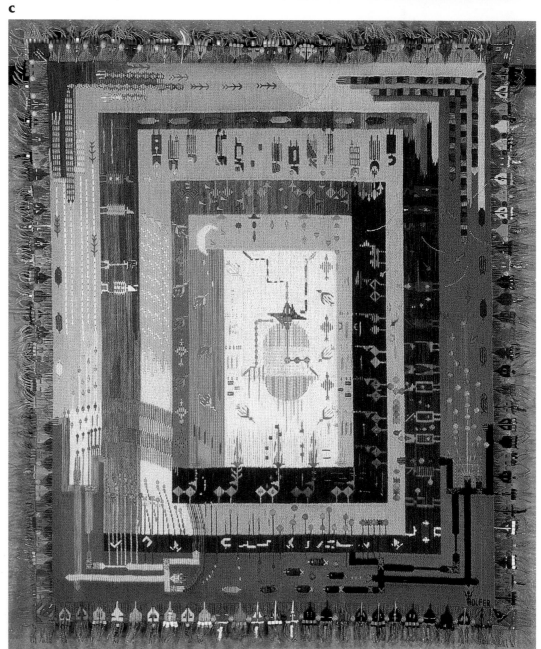

D

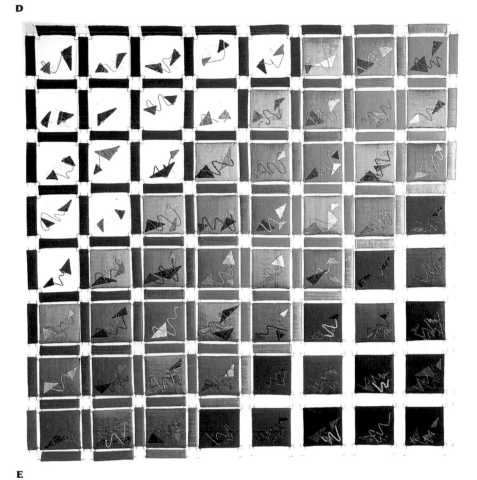

E

D

URSULA GERBER-SENGER
SWITZERLAND

Contemplation

Hand embroidery and appliqué
on transparent acrylic plastic;
130 by 130 cm. Photo: T. Cugini.

E

ASTRID ANDREASEN
DENMARK

Galapagos

Appliqué and stitchery on mixed
fabrics; 207 by 313 cm.

*Visiting a group of islands almost
similar to the Faroe Islands I live on,
but situated at the other side of the
world, was a beautiful and surprising
experience.*

A

JANICE MOEZZI
UNITED STATES

Simin

Free (no hoop) chain, herringbone, and stem stitching using single and double strand embroidery floss; 23 by 18 by 2 in. Photo: Jeffrey Reeder.

My work with thread is chiefly expressionistic, with a preference for the human figure and portraits of people I know.

B

MELINDA MUHN SNYDER
UNITED STATES

Garden Dance

Machine and hand stitching over a painted canvas; 11 by 12-1/2 in. Photo: Geoffrey Carr.

I enjoy using the sewing machine as a drawing tool and find the repetitive motion soothing. The smoothness and texture of the stitching would be impossible for me to duplicate in hand embroidery.

A

B

C

D

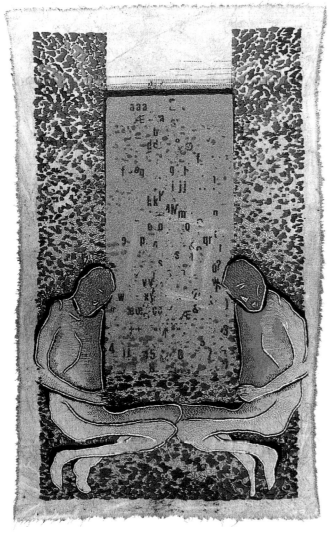

C

THEODORA ELSTON
UNITED STATES

Cycle of Change

Hand embroidery, quilting, and painting on linen; 13 by 16 by 2 in.

During the two years following the Oakland, California firestorm, my emotions and the devastated landscape went through many phases. This is one of a series reflecting some of those changes.

D

SUSANNE KLINKE
GERMANY

Speak Disorder

Embroidery on cotton and paper; 24 by 38 cm.

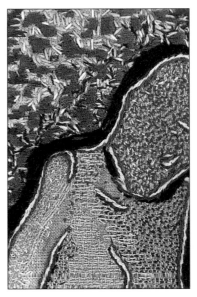

E

PEGGY LOVE
UNITED STATES

Exhilaration

French knots and couching on cotton/linen; 12-1/2 by 12-1/2 by 1 in.

F

MARIBETH BALOGA
UNITED STATES

Family Portrait

Photo silkscreen printing and embroidery; 13-1/2 by 11 in.

E

F

A

A

JANET LESZCZYNSKI
UNITED STATES

Light Impulse

Stitchery using cotton thread and fabric; 3-1/4 by 3-1/8 in. Photo: Steve Grubman.

B

RENIE BRESKIN ADAMS
UNITED STATES

Banatmosphere

Stitching, weaving, and knotless netting on cotton; 7 by 7 in.

I've had bananas on my mind for a long time. They are such a nice shape, like boomerangs and crescent moons.

C

BETH NOBLES
UNITED STATES

Swimmer

Embroidery on cotton; 2-7/8 by 1-3/4 in. Photo: Jon Van Allen.

This was the happy result of difficult circumstances. The flood of '93 came to my town of Riverside, Iowa. Although my house was safe, I was out of work for eight days and it was during that time that I did this piece.

D

GAYLE WILLIAMSON
UNITED STATES

Inter-Forms No. 13

Embroidery and heat transfer on fabric; 5 by 7 in. Photo: Geoffrey Carr.

Viewing frescoes in Italy has influenced my work. Some were cracked and faded; others had been painted over, with an earlier fresco emerging from under a newer layer, and these observations found their way to my pieces.

E

MARGOT LINDSAY
CANADA

November Morning

Couching, straight stitches, and French knots; 20 by 29-1/2 cm. Photo: AK Photos, Grant Kernan.

I've been doing embroidery for 20 years, with an emphasis on free stitchery. The inspiration for my pictures comes from the untouched wilderness of the Saskatchewan Prairie.

B

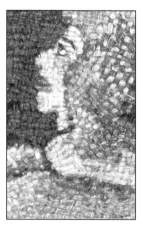

C

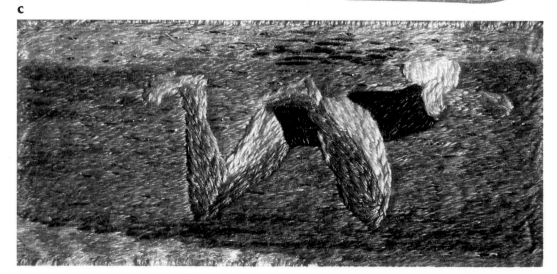

F

LINDA L. BEHAR
UNITED STATES

Vedauwoo Rocks II, Mother and Child

Machine and hand embroidery; 3-3/8 by 5 in.

For years I have made large, wall-size quilts. Recently, I became intrigued with the possibilities of working in miniature, and have only begun to explore a vast visual domain.

G

MARY BERO
UNITED STATES

Lady With Orb

Embroidery and appliqué using cotton, silk, and rayon thread; 4-5/8 by 4-5/8 in. Photo: Wildeman Photographics.

This is part of my continuing series of searching for the self.

D

E

F

G

79

A

J E A N   M A T Z K E
U N I T E D   S T A T E S

Nude Speaking Her Mind

Embroidery, appliqué, and overstitching on velveteen and corduroy; 18-1/2 by 34 in.

This is from a series of embroideries about body language.

B

F E L I C I A
F R A N C E

The Poplars

Embroidery on linen; 61 by 38 cm. Photo: F.Y. Govin.

B

C

ELAINE D. MCBRIDE
UNITED STATES

Adoration of the Good Boy

Basic flat, fill-in, satin single-strand embroidery on muslin; 6 by 6-1/2 in.

I wanted to re-write the wretched dog-obedience-training experience into a positive context.

D

BETH NOBLES
UNITED STATES

The Citizenry

Embroidery on cotton, wood; 4 3/4 by 5-1/2 by 1-1/2 in. Photo: Jon Van Allen.

I made this piece after a friend gave up on trying to get a tourist visa for a Polish pen pal.

E

TOM LUNDBERG
UNITED STATES

Hand Mirror

Embroidery using cotton, silk, and metallic threads on velvet; 12-3/4 by 12-1/2 in. Photo: Colorado State University Photo Services.

A

PAT WELLER
UNITED STATES

Time Flies

Punchneedle embroidery; 31 by
20 by 1 in.

*My embroideries are samplers of my
emotional state. This is about
dichotomies—inside and outside, real
and unreal.*

B

ANNE McKENZIE
NICKOLSON
UNITED STATES

Game of Choice

Machine and hand embroidery
on cotton; 20 by 20-1/2 in.

C

DOBROSLAWA
KOWALEWSKA
POLAND

Addresses

Embroidery on jute; 230 by 115
cm. Photo: Boguslaw
Kowalewski.

*This is the result of thinking about a
family I know—four people living
under the same roof.*

82

D

HERVÉ DUPONT
FRANCE

Yellow Dogs

Oriental stitch on cotton fabric; 40 by 50 cm.

For a man to embroider must seem very eccentric, but I started after visiting the famous Bayeaux tapestry. I am also a glass designer.

E

MILISSA LINK
UNITED STATES

Taming the Green Lion IV

Needlepoint with cotton thread; 9 by 5-5/8 by 5/8 in. Photo: Petronella Ytsma.

My work reflects an interest in archetypal psychology, alchemy, and myth.

F

GILA MADER
ISRAEL

Morning Sunshine

Straight, running, and cross stitches with dyed netting; 100 by 80 cm.

I use the language of textiles to express that the world we wander through is both a rich and strange place.

D

E

F

A

A

ISABELLE FAIDY-CONTREAU
FRANCE

Speed in Vienne

Cross stitch on cotton fabric;
35 by 56 cm.

From a simple stitch mark, I like to play with threads, mix different colors and materials to show that cross stitch can have a new life in textile work.

B

KIRSTY GORTER
AUSTRALIA

Look Mummy, I'm a Tapestry!

Half cross stitch on needlepoint tapestry canvas; 63 by 77 cm.

Nearly all of my inspiration comes from my everyday environment. I work with images which are not normally the focus of attention.

C

ELLY SMITH
UNITED STATES

And Jill Came Tumbling After

Counted thread technique using cotton thread and fabric; 30 by 42 in. Photo: Steve Meltzer.

A comment on marriage: when Jack trips and falls, Jill comes tumbling after.

D

ANNE S. JENNINGS
UNITED STATES

Mosaic for Marjorie

Needlepoint on cotton canvas; 12 by 12 in. Photo: Brent Herridge & Associates.

This is part of a series to celebrate my mother's gorgeous English gardens.

B

C

D

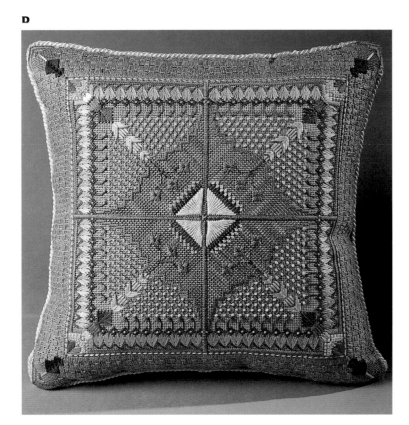

E

F

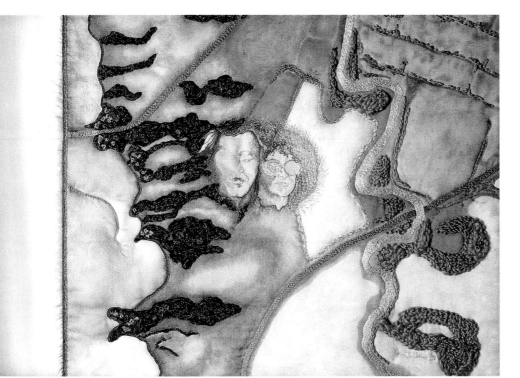

E

THEODORA ZEHNER
UNITED STATES

'80s Sense

Computer generated and manipulated scans translated into 24 count petit point; 9 by 7 in.

I am intrigued by combining the traditional process of petit point with computer technology. The title of this piece refers to the 1980s decade of greed which accelerated the decline of the middle class structure.

F

JONNI TURNER
CANADA

Valley: Illusion

Petit point inlay on dyed and painted ground fabrics with surface embroidery; 24-1/4 by 16-1/4 in. Photo: Patricia Holdsworth.

The big sky tends to overwhelm images in the Saskatchewan Prairie. In this piece, I wanted to change the perspective and to add a human presence that wasn't dwarfed by the landscape.

A

B

C

A

LESLIE MARIE
ULRICH
UNITED STATES

Dress As Pattern

Machine and hand stitching;
11-1/2 by 9 in.

B

TILLEKE SCHWARZ
THE NETHERLANDS

"I have known them all"

Freestyle, cross stitch embroidery, and textile paint on linen;
50 by 50 cm.

*This work deals with my background
and the Jewish culture. The title refers
to a comment of my mother about
people she knew who died in World
War II.*

C

MÁRIA DANIELOVÁ
CZECH REPUBLIC

Crystals

Bobbin lace using linen and
cotton; 150 by 40 cm.

*The space in my two-dimensional
work is an illusion.*

Two Dimensions

· · · · · · ·

Previous Page

ANN HARTLEY
UNITED STATES

This Fragile Earth: Rebirth

Mixed media collage with copper, photo transfers, and acrylics; 20 by 30 in.

A

JOY SAVILLE
UNITED STATES

Late October

Pieced, stitched, and constructed using cotton, linen, and silk; 63 by 62 in. Photo: William Taylor.

One hundred and three shades of fabric are used; each adds its own distinctive texture and ability to absorb or reflect light.

B

DONNA RHAE MARDER
UNITED STATES

Mending

Sewing of burnt coffee filters; 32 by 46 in. Photo: David Caras.

I have been sewing scraps of paper into objects for years. This body of work is about surviving and making do.

A

B

C

D

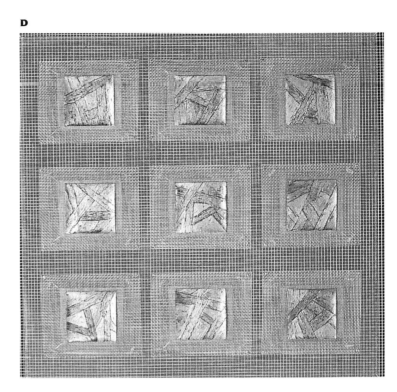

E

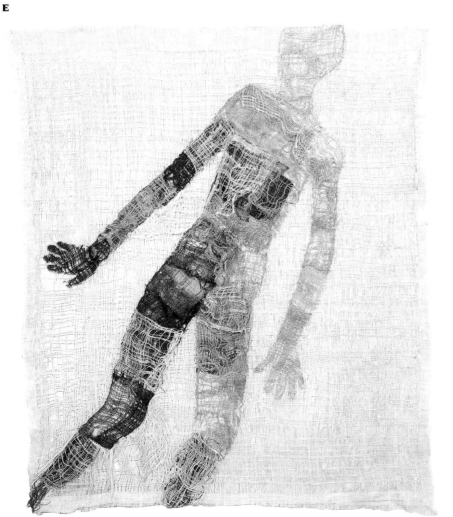

C

KATHLEEN HOLMES
UNITED STATES

Private Garden

Mixed media on canvas; 28 by 21 in. Photo: Robert Nelson.

D

ANNE MARIE KENNY
UNITED STATES

Woven II Industrial Quilt

Mixed media assemblage; 36 by 37 in. Photo: Jack Bingham.

Wire cloth, fiberglass, acrylic paintings, and wire "thread" were used in making this piece. The contrasts of hand made and machine made are designed to complement each other as well as provoke the controversy surrounding the way things of value are made.

E

ZUZANA RUDAVSKA
UNITED STATES

Figure

Mixed techniques and dyeing of burlap; 65 by 60 in. Photo: Gary Keith Griffin.

Interplay between solid and flexible materials, and openness through which air and light may move are my primary concerns.

A

B

C

A

C H R I S T I E L.
D U N N I N G
UNITED STATES

Domestic Textiles - Dinner for Two

Pieced, woven, stitched, embroidered, dyed, painted, and screen printed cotton; 15 by 15 in.

B

M A R Y C A T H E R I N E
L A M B
UNITED STATES

Saint Anthony's Torment

Appliquéd, pieced, and quilted commercial cotton and metallic fabrics; 48 by 68 in. Photo: David Browne.

Saint Anthony lived as a hermit, alone in a cave for 20 years and, not surprisingly, was tormented by visions of demons. He resisted their tortures with the strength of his faith. The metaphor of facing personal demons and maintaining clarity through one's own convictions is a compelling one.

D

E

C

PHYLLIS CERATTO
EVANS
UNITED STATES

Siesta in Riomaggiore

Japanese kimono silk fused to canvas and mounted on rigid board; 28 by 39 in. Photo: Wally Hampton, Photography.

D

CHARLENE K.
NEMEC
UNITED STATES

Ordinary Language

Woven and stitched cotton and rayon; 21 by 26 in.

My work explores vulnerability. The house images are symbolic of the body. The crumbling house in which the central figure stands represents the deteriorating mind, the gradual loss of control as one struggles to maintain sanity.

E

SALLY A. SELLERS
UNITED STATES

Home Body

Machine appliqué using commercial fabrics; 56 by 59 in. Photo: David Browne.

This image arose when I was faced with the painful realization that I could no longer take care of my 7-year-old daughter's medical needs at home. Her (permanent) move to the hospital violated my maternal instinct at the deepest level.

A

A

KIT LONEY
UNITED STATES

Woven Torso: After 12th C.
Auvergne Crucifix

Torn and reconstructed weaving
and drawing with rayon, wool,
silk, and cotton; 65 by 23 in.

After it is torn, the paper drawing be-
comes, like yarn, a weaving material.

B

LAURIE DILL-
KOCHER
UNITED STATES

Nature's Palette 7.0

Boundweave, tapestry, machine
stitching, and painting of cotton, wool, and silk; 45 by 57 in.
Photo: Thomas Kocher.

In the past few years, I have come to
realize that all the things that happen
to or around me—the joys and the
sorrows—are reflected in my work.
Most recently, the death of a friend
manifested itself in the wrapped and
bent elements that are contained in
the "Nature's Palette" series.

B

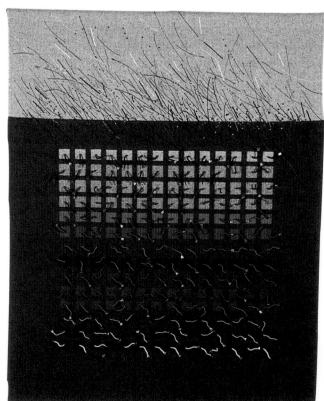

C

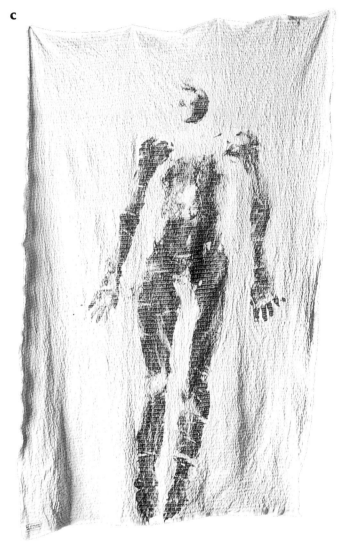

C

L INDSAY O BERMEYER
U NITED S TATES

Clinical Diagnosis: Wilm's Tumor

Computerized machine embroidery, hand writing, stamping on discarded hospital sheet; 43-1/4 by 72 in. Photo: John Phelan.

My memories of a childhood cancer are obliterated by medical jargon. The inscription of my body by the hospital/medical institution confines and isolates me.

D

L ORE L INDENFELD
U NITED S TATES

Echoes of Sado Island 2

Stitching and drawing using Japanese paper, nylon netting, and polyester interfacing; 12 by 18 in.

The beauty of rock formations, weathered wood, and cut stone on Sado Island, Japan, sharpened my awareness of natural forms.

E

J ACQUELINE G OVIN
F RANCE

Still Life and Poem

Dyeing, painting, embroidery, appliqué, patchwork, and weaving on silk; 46 by 33 cm. Photo: F.Y. Govin.

D

E

A

PATRICIA MALARCHER
UNITED STATES

Tergiversation

Machine, hand stitching, painting, and collage using Mylar; 66 by 60 in. Photo: D. James Dee.

Frequently I borrow formats from textile history, such as the quilt and the prayer rug. I want my work to allude, in a non-specific way, to the use of textiles as accessories to ritual and celebration, either as architectural embellishment, vesture, or ritual accessories.

B

KATHERINE KNAUER
UNITED STATES

Desert Stormy Weather

Pieced, stenciled, and airbrushed cotton; 78 by 78 in. Photo: Myron Miller.

This deals specifically with the oil well fires and the deliberate eco-vandalism during the Gulf War of 1991. The flags of both the U.S. and Iraq incorporate stars and stripes; I distorted those shapes and used them throughout this piece.

C

DAVID WEIDIG
UNITED STATES

Kozmic Beat No. 3

Interlacing, stitching, assemblage, painting, and collage of paper and nylon; 70-1/2 by 43 in.

When chaos and order met to discuss the formation of the universe, the result was a delicate fabric woven of time and dimension in an exaggerated twill.

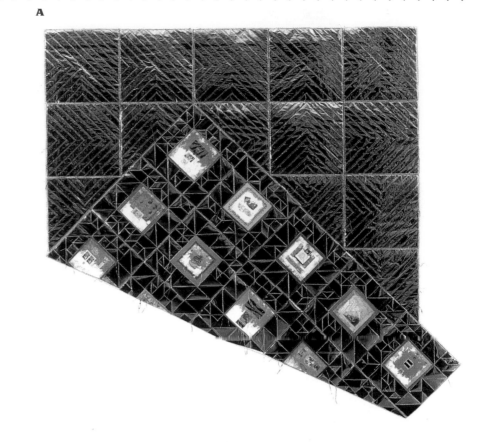

94

C

D

LESLIE NOBLER
FARBER
UNITED STATES

Sawtooth

Computer-aided imaging, sewing, heat transfer dyeing, and painting on paper and vinyl; 26 by 20 in.

The work is about blending so-called high- and low-tech processes. I continually experiment to try to develop better "desk top" textile-to-computer (and vice versa) techniques.

E

KATHLEEN BALEJA,
JUDY MORNINGSTAR,
ELAINE ROUNDS
CANADA

Cosmic Connections

Weaving, quilting, and stained glass; 30 by 30 in.

Three creative heads are better than one. We have been collaborating since 1993.

D

E

A

KAREN OLESEN JAKSE
UNITED STATES

Nowhere For A Tree To Go

Crackle weave structure with antique kimono silk as the weft; 15 by 55 in. Photo: Wayne Torborg.

This was inspired by author Diane Ackerman's description of nature's response to the approach of winter.

B

I. WOJCIECH JASKOLKA
POLAND

Text-BC

Woven using linen, cotton, silk, wool, and copper wire; 31 by 36 cm.

C

MORGAN ELIZABETH CLIFFORD
UNITED STATES

Pathways

Woven/brocade, printed and painted warp using linen/silk; 72 by 14 in. Photo: Peter Lee.

I want my pieces to remind the viewer more of a dish towel or tablecloth than of a painting.

D

BHAKTI ZIEK
UNITED STATES

Up/Down

Painted warp, lampas pick-up weave with mixed fibers; 49 by 56 in. Photo: Tracey Howard.

Individual threads become a whole cloth; individual circles become a united design; individual lives play out the universal drama.

A

B

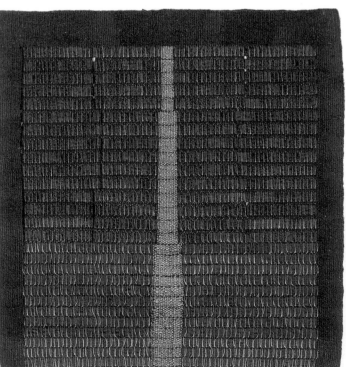

C

D

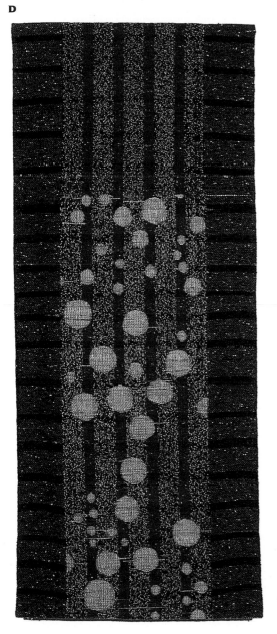
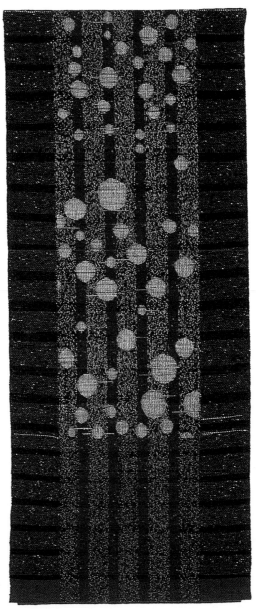

A

FRAN CUTRELL RUTKOVSKY
UNITED STATES

Family Values

Weaving and collage of printed materials on a cotton warp; 13 by 12-1/2 in. Photo: Richard Brunck.

I'm intrigued by the misuse of information, distortion of facts, mistaken assumptions, and superficial appearances. My work involves dissecting and restructuring information so that it becomes nothing more than a visual component.

B

ANNE-MARIE BERTAND
FRANCE

Gable Wall No. 2

Appliqué, collage, dyeing, painting, and embroidery on cotton; 65 by 54 cm.

C

WLODZIMIERZ CYGAN
POLAND

You Can See

Woven jute and sisal; 165 by 180 cm.

What you see is what you get.

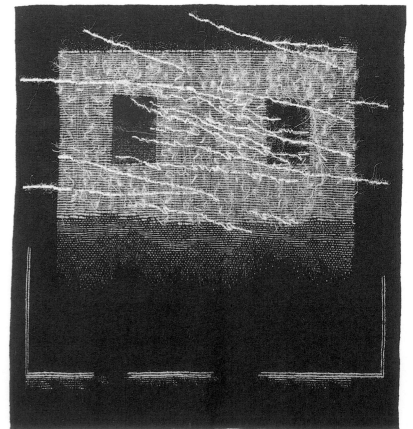

D

D

L E S L E Y   M I T C H I S O N
ENGLAND

Three X Basque

Woven and embroidered cotton/silk/polyester; 38 by 32 cm.

The design is meant to evoke the qualities found in the layered, structured elements of Victorian corsetry.

E

D A V I D   B .   B R A C K E T T
UNITED STATES

Three Stages

Space dyed supplemental warp, polychromatic and photo screen printing of cotton, rayon, and monofilament; 106 by 80 in.

Our daily world is filled with chance occurrences, and I am intrigued by the way natural forces shape these random happenings into pattern and order.

E

A

VICKIE VIPPERMAN
UNITED STATES

A Month of Sundays

Plain weave with a cotton warp and paper weft; 60 by 46 in. Photo: Chromatics, Inc.

This was woven using the headlines of 31 consecutive Sunday newspapers.

B

MARIE WESTERMAN
UNITED STATES

Fault Lines: Vanishing Point

Multi-layer weave with linen; 36 by 60 in. Photo: Judy Horner Photography.

The word "fault" conveys more than a break in the earth's crust. We need to remind ourselves that nothing is certain or lasts forever, and that our faults can bring our lives down around our heads.

C

W. LOGAN FRY
UNITED STATES

Microchip Series 2: Poly

Finnweave using two-ply wool; 35 by 37 in. Photo: Jean Schnell.

The series is based on the metal mask of an AT&T Bell Laboratories MAC-8 microprocessor.

D

ORIANE STENDER
UNITED STATES

Occupied Territory

Supplementary weft pick-up using rayon and cotton; 19-1/2 by 17 in.

When reading a film article, this sentence jumped out: "Mr. De Niro plays a police photographer who saves Bill Murray's life and as a reward is given Uma Thurman for a week." This plot description has become commonplace in the way women are represented in mainstream films.

E

VIRGINIA DAVIS
UNITED STATES

Optical 1

Warp and weft painting of linen yarn; 38 by 38 in. Photo: Elijah Cobb.

I literally weave painter's linen canvas similar to the sort that can be purchased from artists' material suppliers. Ikat technique—dyeing and painting the yarn before weaving—enables color and image to be embedded in the woven structure and locked into the canvas.

A

B

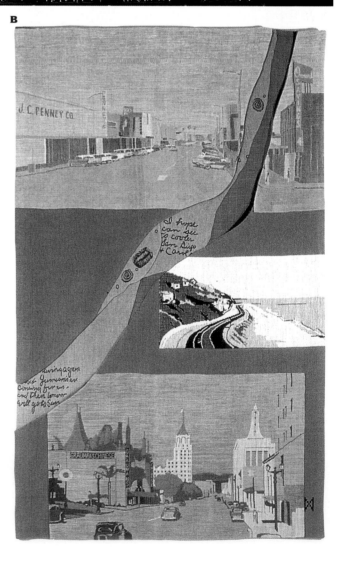

C

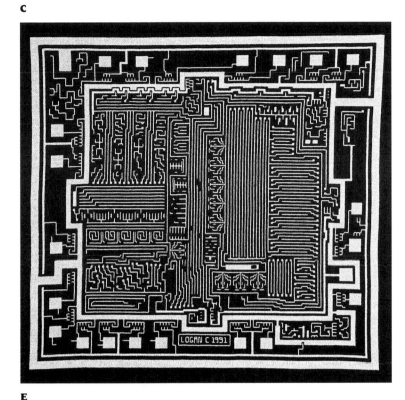

D

E

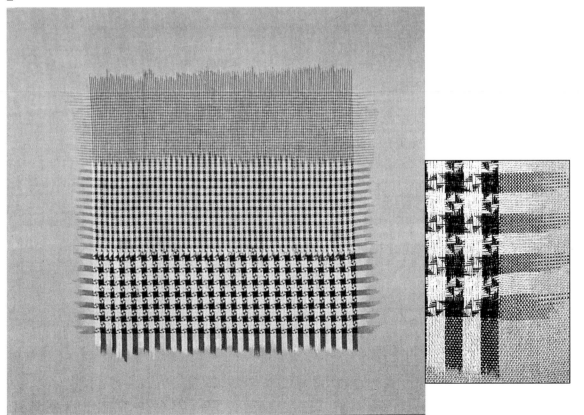

A

B

A

JUDITH POXSON
FAWKES
UNITED STATES

Campanile, Capella & Cloister

Inlay technique using linen; 79 by 44 in. Photo: Bill Bachhuber; collection of Stanford University.

B

BETTY VERA
UNITED STATES

Memories

Painted warp, discontinuous tapestry-woven wefts, broken twill weaves, and embroidery using cotton and linen; 60 by 63 in. Photo: Adam Reich.

This is based on my memories of a visit to Grand Manan Island, New Brunswick.

C

CATRINA SUTTER
NEW ZEALAND

Together - Alone

Weaving, dye painting, and embroidery of linen and silk; 69 by 54 cm. Photo: Lawrence Aeberhardt.

This is my impression of a lunar eclipse.

D

CYNDY BARBONE
UNITED STATES

In the Garden II

Inlay, double weave, and brocade using cotton, silk, and rayon; 60 by 40 in. Photo: Joseph Levy.

Integrating technique and pictorial imagery so they merge and reinforce one another has been a constant goal in my work.

C

D

103

A

LIZ PULOS
UNITED STATES

Constellation

Double weave pick-up with mercerized cotton; 39 by 31 in. Photo: Steve Ostrowski.

B

CAMERON TAYLOR-BROWN
UNITED STATES

On the Fringe/Diagonal Path #2

Weaving, stitching, and painting of linen, cotton, and rayon; 48 by 64 in. Photo: Q.

I am intrigued by the interaction of light/shadow and color/pattern which is capable with the woven structure.

C

KERSTIN ÅSLING-SUNDBERG
Sweden

Square III

Damask weave with cotton and flax; 90 by 90 cm.

D

CATHERINE BARRITT
UNITED STATES

Temple

Double warp painted and pick-up weave technique with cotton and nylon; 20 by 20-1/4 in. Photo: Bill Finney.

The central form appears frequently in my work. Here it represents spirit, soul, the eternal flame within each being, each temple.

E

ELIZABETH G. KUHN
UNITED STATES

Heritage II

Double weave pick-up of dyed cotton; 27 by 27 in.

The occupations and deeds of my family are depicted here. Women are represented in the center, men in the border.

F

BRENDA J. STULTZ
UNITED STATES

Interlacement IV

Double weave of cotton; 53 by 53 in.

A

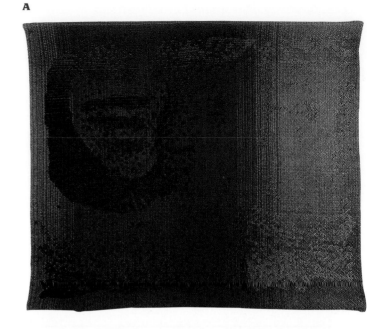

B

C

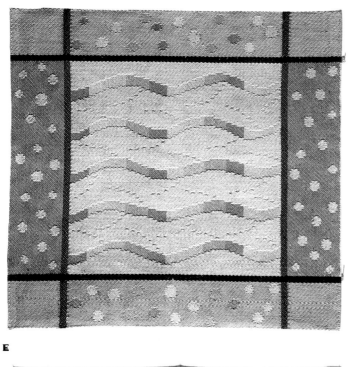

D

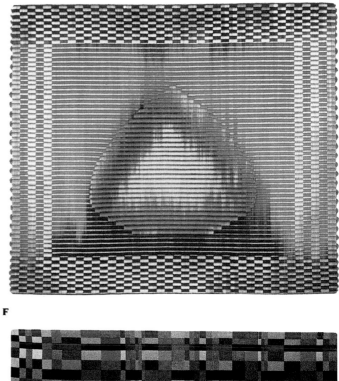

E

F

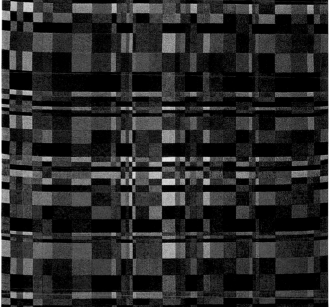

A

FUYUKO MATSUBARA
UNITED STATES

The Transition I

Warp and weft painting with
hand plied linen, cotton, silk,
and rayon; 29 by 18 in.

B

ANNEMARIE BUCHMANN-GERBER
CANADA

A *Piece of Daily Life* No. 2

Painting, appliqué, collage, and
stitchery on linen; 103 by 111
cm. Photo: A.K. Photos.

C

DIANE BEVAN FIELDS
UNITED STATES

High Road

Ikat dyed and woven cotton; 44
by 90 in. Photo: Gary L.
Warnimont.

D

KARIN NEBEL
SWITZERLAND

AND

MARIETTE WOLBERT
THE NETHERLANDS

**Experimental study for curtains:
*Atlas***

Ikat, double weaving, transfer
printing, painting of cotton and
linen.

*Since 1992, we have worked together
under the name, Dutch.Swiss &
Partners. Karin's specialty is printed
design and Mariette's is weaving.*

E

BARBARA SCHULMAN
UNITED STATES

A Twenty-Five Hour Day

Plaited and painted cotton; 100
by 50 in. Photo: Doug Van De
Zande.

A

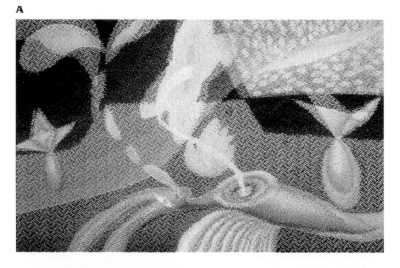

B

C

D

E

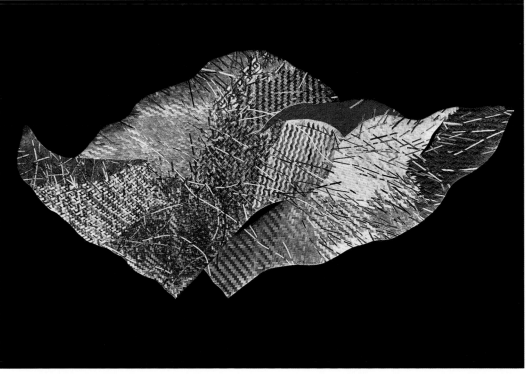

JANET CARIJA BRANDT
UNITED STATES

Village Wedding

Hooked wool; 26 by 35 in.

This could've been my great grand-parents' European village wedding.

B

LOIS BLACKBURN
ENGLAND

The Bath

Hooked recycled fabrics; 60 by 80 cm.

I wish to reconcile what are often thought of as distinct boundaries between fine art, design, and craft to produce work that incorporates aspects of all three.

C

NANCY MARTINEAU
UNITED STATES

Her Checkered Past

Hooked and dyed wool; 46 by 52 in. Photo: Shelly Fowler.

This is one in a series that was inspired by patterns in men's swimming trunks.

D

NEL RAND
UNITED STATES

Catching the Wind

Hooked wool; 32 by 29 in. Photo: Frank Engel.

Since 1992, I have been painting the faces of my favorite contemporary artists using their obituary photos. I began to dream about these faces being hooked in wool, I believe because I needed to linger with them longer than it took to paint them.

E

ROSLYN LOGSDON
UNITED STATES

Class at Green Mountain

Hooked wool; 25 by 18 in. Photo: Linda Zandler.

Within a limited palette, there are still many variations. Working on this piece was like working out a puzzle.

F

CAROLINE ANDERSON
UNITED STATES

Back When The Sky Was The Limit

Hooked wool embellished with glass beads; 28 by 21-1/2 in. Photo: Chromatics.

This piece celebrates one fine afternoon I spent at the top of a mountain.

A

Susan M. Clark
CANADA

White Male Rug

Hooked mixed, recycled fibers;
89 by 235 cm.

*I began this piece at a monastery
artists' colony. The monks were very
puzzled.*

B

Jan Whitaker
UNITED STATES

House-a-Tumble

Hand hooked wool; 36 by 26 in.

A

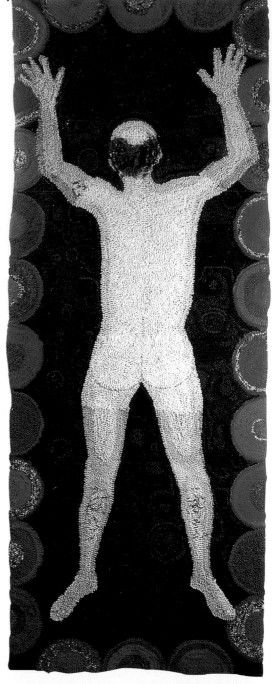

B

C

C

PRUDENCE
MATTHEWS
UNITED STATES

Free Loader on the St. Lawrence

Hooked and dyed wool; 25 by
48 in. Photo: Robert Matthews.

D

REBECCA CLARK
KNUDSEN
UNITED STATES

*The Work To Which I Have Been
Called*

Continuous loop primitive
hooking with burlap and wool;
42 by 84 in.

*This rug was inspired by the Mormon
prophet, Alma.*

E

PEG IRISH
UNITED STATES

Emerging Crocus

Hooked wool, embellished with
ribbon and suede; 19-1/2 by 18-
1/2 in. Photo: Jim Irish.

*This was begun in response to the cre-
ative process challenge in Fiberarts
Magazine. It gave me the impetus to
try a variety of materials and design
combinations.*

F

ANN WINTERLING
UNITED STATES

Alice in the Queen's Garden

Hooked dyed wool; 53 by 53 in.
Photo: Garth Winterling, courtesy Peg Irish.

*I started this as a floral, but the over-
sized tree peonies inspired me to add
Alice to the garden.*

D

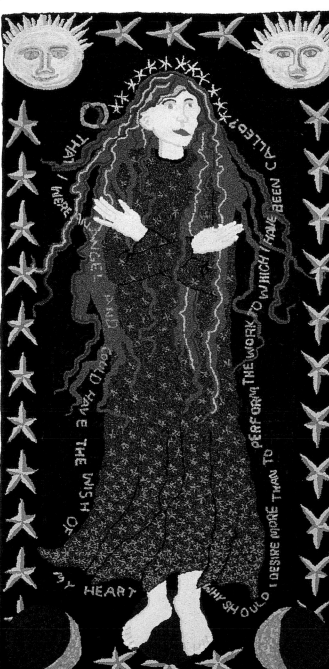

E

F

A

FLO BARRY
UNITED STATES

Fun Down Under

Stretched, painted, and dyed canvas; 47 by 67 in.

B

HEATHER ALLEN
UNITED STATES

Paradise II

Dyed and painted cotton rag rug; 42 by 70-1/2 in. Photo: John Lucas.

C

WENDY WAHL
UNITED STATES

Charted Course

Hand tufted wool and silk; 66 by 88 in. Photo: Ric Murray.

D

AMANDA SEARS
UNITED STATES

Tea Party

Tufted dyed raffia; 38 by 71 in.

Akin to stitching, the tufting process allows for spontaneity and fluidity that suits my style of working.

E

MARTHA DONOVAN OPDAHL
UNITED STATES

Persian Light - Prayer Rug Series #2

Ikat dyeing and tufting of wool; 41-1/4 by 72-1/2 in.

The idea behind my work can be expressed as a tension between all that is ordered, deliberate, calculated, predictable, and controlled on one hand, and all that is spontaneous, random, exhuberant, chaotic, and improvisational on the other.

A

B

112

D

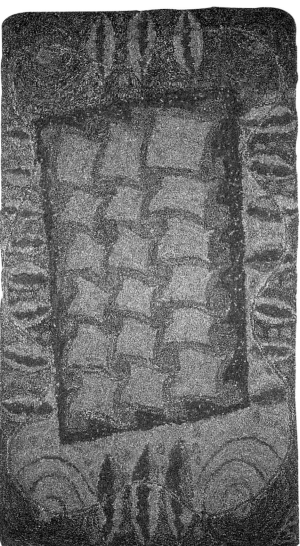

E

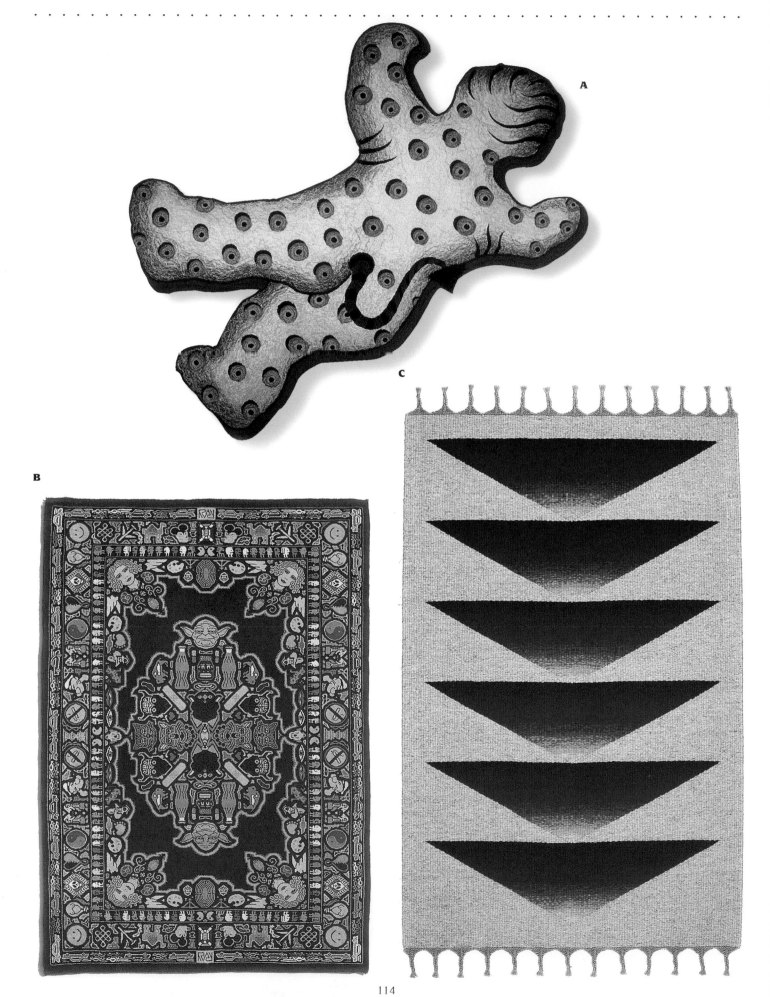

A

C

B

114

D

A

JOHN L. SKAU
UNITED STATES

Pelt

Looped pile technique with wool and silk yarns, fabric collage of wool fabric; 95 by 103 in.

This is a portrait of a brother who died from complications that arose from an infection with the AIDS virus.

B

RAY VARNBUHLER
UNITED STATES

East Meets West

Hand knotted wool pile, cotton warp; 43 by 65 in.

C

PAT ADAMS
CANADA

Untitled

Kilim technique using wool and linen; 81 by 130 cm. Photo: AK Photos, Grant Kernan.

D

KATE MARTIN
UNITED STATES

Spontaneous Combustion

Punch hooked wool; 54 by 36 in. Photo: Joe Coca.

The world is defined by relationships I am fascinated by the invisible chemistry that fuels these relationships and often leads to a "fiery" result.

E

JANE KIDD
CANADA

Temple Series Carpet #1

Hand punched wool; 54 by 84 in. Photo: John Dean.

These limited edition carpets are designed by me and hand made by the best artisans in the Orient.

E

A

GLORIA E. CROUSE
UNITED STATES

Diverse-Directions

Rug hooking variations using wool and silver metallics, embellished with metal elements; 144 by 120 in.

Although fiber is my love, I like to incorporate elements from my background of working with metal.

B

MARGARET CUSACK
UNITED STATES

Hands

Machine appliquéd and airbrushed fabrics; 108 by 144 in. Photo: Ron Breland; collection of The Culinary Institute of America.

C

BILL RAFNEL
UNITED STATES

Untitled Commission

Damask weaving of pearl cotton; 15 by 4 ft. Photo: Corell Blanco Studio.

B

A

C

THREE DIMENSIONS

· · · · · · ·

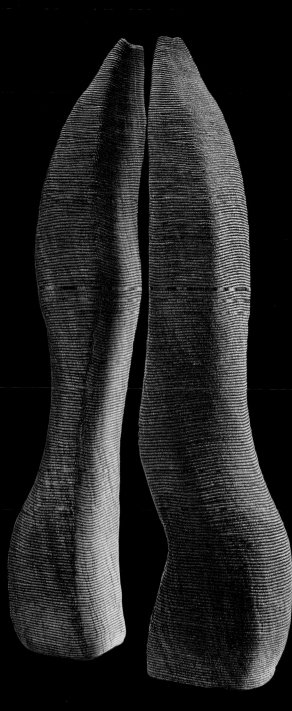

Previous Page

JANE SAUER
UNITED STATES

Alignment

Knotted and painted waxed linen; 13 by 30 by 4 in. Photo: Mark Katzman.

I'm interested in making the negative space be as integral to the work as the forms that comprise the positive space.

A

DONA LOOK
UNITED STATES

Basket #913

Wrapped and sewn white birch bark; 10-1/2 by 11 by 10-1/2 in. Photo: Dedra Walls.

B

CHAR WISS
UNITED STATES

Dream City

Coiling of waxed linen on a telephone wire core; 7-1/2 by 7-1/2 by 7 in. Photo: Mary A. Root.

This was a reaction to temporarily living in Washington, D.C.—"dream city."

A

B

C

D

E

C

MARILYN MOORE
UNITED STATES

Reversal in Red

Coiling with polished hemp and waxed linen; 7-1/2 by 3-1/2 by 7-1/2 in. Photo: John Moore.

D

PATTI LECHMAN
UNITED STATES

Asti

Knotted nylon; 4-1/4 by 5-1/2 by 4 in. Photo: Charles Woodliff.

The vessel—the archetypal female form—has been central to my work for more than 20 years, whether made of clay or fiber. Both materials are associated with Neolithic civilizations which produced vessels to store and carry grain, water, wine…life-giving substances.

E

ELINOR J. SPLITTER
UNITED STATES

S.W. Viking

3 rod wale weave, coiling, laminating, and painting of reed; 17 by 16 by 17 in. Photo: Randall Smith.

My forms are inspired by the timeless struggle we all experience in our lives: to be our unique selves or to blend in anonymously with the masses.

A

CAROL D. WESTFALL
UNITED STATES

This Crowded Planet

Weaver's knots on dyed plastic paper; 6 by 6 by 6 in. Photo: D. James Dee.

As I made the knots for this piece, I saw the kanji which translates to "man." When I balled them all together, I felt the crush of humanity in our cities.

A

B

B

KATHLEEN PEELEN KREBS
UNITED STATES

Coiled Torrey Pine Needle Vessel

Pine needles and waxed linen; 9 by 12 in. diameter. Photo: G.F. Krebs.

C

FLO HOPPE
UNITED STATES

Fukui

Twining and painting on rattan and handmade paper; 10 by 6 by 3 in. Photo: John C. Keys.

D

D

J ACKIE A BRAMS
U NITED S TATES

Blue Ode to Judy O

Straight plaiting and painting
on paper; 13 by 5 by 13 in.
Photo: Charley Freiberg.

*Papers are painted, embellished, then
stripped with a pasta machine to form
them into basketmaking material.*

E

J O S TEALEY
U NITED S TATES

Ritual Dance

Twining and collage with reed
and handmade paper; 10 by 26
by 10 in. Photo: Jim Curly.

F

J EANNINE G ORESKI
U NITED S TATES

Atlanta Passions

Bead weaving with glass beads;
6 by 4-1/2 by 2-1/2 in. Photo:
John Bonath.

A

PRISCILLA
HENDERSON
UNITED STATES

Woman as Mender

Rib construction, wickerweave, painting, and lacquering with hard maple and rattan; 32 by 7 by 32 in.

B

MELINDA **W**EST
UNITED STATES

Free-Standing Mounted Maple Pouch

Folding, plaiting, and lashing with maple and cedar bark; 20 by 5 by 4-1/2 in. Photo: Wally Hampton.

Bark folding has been practiced by northwest aboriginal cultures for centuries. I am constantly inspired by the work of these predecessors.

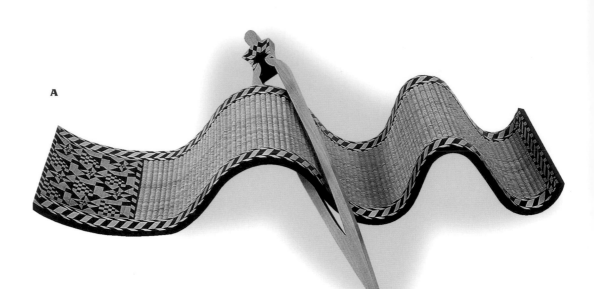

A

B

C

D

E

C

DARLENE NGUYEN-ELY
UNITED STATES

Tuna: 21st Century Tribal Series

Wrapping and stitching with kozo, raffia, palm frond, reed, and hardware cloth; 53 by 12 by 53 in. Photo: Richard Niscior.

As a native of Vietnam, I was awed by the modern industrial landscape of the United States. The works in this series reflect my attempts to reconcile the traditional Vietnamese culture with modern American culture.

D

MARY MERKEL-HESS
UNITED STATES

Shell

Molded paper; 20 by 13 by 23 in.

E

ILSE BOLLE
UNITED STATES

Bridge to Paradise III

Handmade paper and willow couched onto grids and knotted together; 32 by 64 by 15 in. Photo: Dennis Sullivan.

123

A

S HARON R OBINSON
U NITED S TATES

Summer Eve

Stiffened tissue paper and loom woven seed beads; 6 by 6 by 6 in. Photo: Bruce Shippee.

B

B IRD R OSS
U NITED S TATES

Black & Gold Jar © 1993

Machine pieced and stitched vintage and modern silk; 12 by 12 by 8 in. Photo: Harper Fritch.

My vessels evolved from a desire to create baskets using the materials I most crave (fabric and thread) and a technique about which I am knowledgeable (machine sewing).

C

J UDY M ULFORD
U NITED S TATES

Wedding Basket

Knotless netting, photo transfers, and dyeing on a gourd; 7 by 13-1/2 in. diameter.

Being a wife, mother, and "Nana" have been the most important things in my life. Nurturing is what I know best. I use images of women and children because I want to validate the importance of the family unit and the values and morals it nurtures.

D

J ENNIFER D YER
U NITED S TATES

Tower III

Woven and painted aluminum; 8 by 13-1/2 by 7 in.

E

Z OE M ORROW
U NITED S TATES

Greentower

Woven shredded U.S. currency; 2 by 8-1/2 by 2 in. Photo: Charles H. Jenkins III.

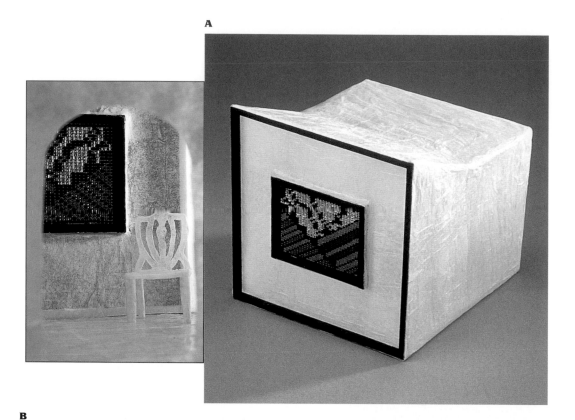

A

B

C

D

E

125

A

HELEN WEBB
ENGLAND

Willow Balls

Traditional basketmaking techniques with fresh willow; 20 to 60 cm. diameter.

It was not easy to get the fresh willow woven into a round shape!

B

DIANNE STANTON
UNITED STATES

Facets

Twining and lashing using elm bark; 11 by 11 by 11 in. Photo: J. David Congalton.

The elm bark rim on this basket has the corky bark left on—an attempt to "put back" part of the tree.

C

CAROLA FARTHING
UNITED STATES

Random Blips

Embellished and dyed gourd; 10 by 10 in. diameter. Photo: Gugger Petter.

Gourds are both magical and grounding to me.

D

BILLIE RUTH SUDDUTH
UNITED STATES

Fibonacci IV

Twill and reverse twill construction with cut and walnut dyed reed; 17 by 14-1/2 by 17-1/2 in. Photo: Melva Calder.

E

MARILYN J. SHARP
UNITED STATES

In-then-Out

Wrapped, twined paper rush; 12 by 12 by 12 in. Photo: R. Sharp.

F

BARBARA SHAW BRINSON
UNITED STATES

Swift Flight

Engraving, drawing, painting, pine needle coiling on gourd; 11 by 11 by 11 in.

A

B

C

D

E

F

A

JANET KUEMMERLEIN
UNITED STATES

Free-form Fish Bowl

Formed and painted felt; 25 by
14 in. Photo: Duane Scott.

B

SALLY KNIGHT
UNITED STATES

City Bowl

Collage, stitching, and drawing
on fabric; 11 by 5 by 11 in.
Photo: Stephen Ostrowski.

*Patterned fabrics often hold secret
treasures for us. We just need to look
for the "pattern within the pattern" to
find them.*

C

RENI TAJIMA
JAPAN

Morning Dew

Machine embroidery on
organdy; 23 by 21 by 21 cm.

*I choose to make containers because
the form is universal and can be
found in every culture from primitive
to contemporary times.*

A

B

C

D

D

KEIKO TAKEDA
JAPAN

Urban Air V

Dyed and woven rattan; 12 by 10 by 6, 7 by 17 by 7, and 17 by 5 by 6 cm. Photo: Yoshihito Nakao.

E

MAGGIE HENTON
ENGLAND

Untitled

Dyed, plaited, and painted cane; 16-1/2 by 20 by 9 in.

E

A

JOHN E. MCGUIRE
UNITED STATES

Kiva

Plaited black ash; 12 by 12 by 16 in. Photo: Dale Duchesne.

This is an interpretation of the Pueblo culture's secret room devoted to religious ceremonies.

B

NORIKO TAKAMIYA
JAPAN

Cast Grass

Wrapped ramie; 30 by 30 by 30 cm.

I have found that wrapping around a mold is a useful way to make complicated forms.

A

B

C

C

MARY ZENA
UNITED STATES

Bloomin' Stitches

Machine stitching on linen; 9 by 9 by 3 in. Photo: Geoffrey Carr.

Making this stuff has been the most fun I've had in my 71 years!

D

MARLA BRILL
UNITED STATES

Cat's Cradle II

Molded, laminated, and painted handmade paper; 17 by 14 by 9 in. Photo: Phil Goldman Photography.

The vessel form both intrigues and seduces my consciousness, and it provides me with the most satisfying vehicle of personal expression.

E

LOIS SCHKLAR
CANADA

Form: Open

Fused, machine stitched, and painted burlap; 27-1/2 by 7-1/2 by 10 in. Photo: Alex Neumann.

My challenge is to discover ways to actualize my feelings and thoughts in forms which evoke emotional and intellectual responses.

D

E

A

NORMA MINKOWITZ
UNITED STATES

Box

Mixed media techniques using fiber, paper, wood, and paint; 8 by 8-1/2 by 16 in. Photo: Bobby Hansson.

My focus is to manipulate linear elements into personal statements, and to enclose and expose a mysteriousness that invites contemplation.

B

PETER GENTENAAR
THE NETHERLANDS

Organic Life

Etching on unspun, beaten linen; 20 by 14 by 2-1/2 cm. Photo: Pat Gentenaar.

Man as a part of nature sometimes feels strange.

C

SUSIE COLQUITT
UNITED STATES

Elevated Notions

Simple handsewn construction with reclaimed zippers; 8-1/2 by 6-1/2 by 8-1/2 in. Photo: Jim Andes.

D

ZHU WEI
CHINA

Textile Construction

Free woven cotton and polyester; 20 by 17 by 17 cm.

E

JEFFREY T. RUTLEDGE
UNITED STATES

Untitled

Interlaced and painted strips of cotton; 28 by 42 by 6 in. Photo: Mary Rezny.

A

B

C

D

132

E

F

SYLVIA PTAK
CANADA

Veiled Connections

Mixed media with fabric, acetate, Japanese paper, assorted wire; 62 by 43 by 10 in. Photo: Lorne Fromer.

The woven wire acts as a subtle divider between the image and the viewer, just as memories are sometimes clear and other times elusive.

G

MARIO ALBERTO FERNÁNDEZ
ARGENTINA

Agonia Amazonica

Mixed media using wicker, industrial fibers, and feathers; 105 by 205 by 10 cm.

F

G

A

A

ERICA LICEA-KANE
UNITED STATES

Underneath It All

Sewn and painted hand woven wool panels, printed rice paper; 35 by 35 by 1 in. Photo: Gordon Bernstein.

After many years of doing highly decorative work, I have recently returned to the loom. This came after a personal revelation in which I recognized that textile processes are very much a part of my creative existence.

B

JODI KANTER
UNITED STATES

Garden Wall

Loom woven linen and metallic yarns, construction; 48 by 72 by 8 in.

As an apprentice weaver in Europe, I was drawn to the great buildings where I sketched, photographed, and observed the interiors and exteriors. Architecture is frequently a partner to my work.

C

ROSITA JOHANSON
CANADA

Millennium

Machine embroidery and mixed media; 12-5/8 by 10-5/8 by 1 in. Photo: Lenscape Incorporated.

This is my interpretation of an Egyptian king's burial chamber.

B

C

D

E

D

HEIDI DARR-HOPE
UNITED STATES

Pathway Icon: Interior Knowledge

Copper tooling, embroidery, drawing, painting, and collage using paper, copper foil, and found objects; 11 by 12 by 1-1/2 in.

My work is influenced by the Mexican tradition of Retablos painting as well as the Byzantine tradition of creating religious icons. Both of these traditions create objects which serve as links between the earthly viewer and the spiritual realm.

E

JAN JANEIRO
UNITED STATES

Ropetricks

Woven and painted raffia; 36 by 24 by 2 in. Photo: Pat Pollard.

This is about binding parts of one's life together—making a whole of one's public and private lives.

135

A

LOIS MORRISON
UNITED STATES

Japanese Rabbits

Appliqué, reverse appliqué, and woodcut rubbings on Japanese kimono fabrics; 6 by 8-3/4 in.

This is my gun control book. Each left-hand page has a hand gun pointing at the ever-fleeing rabbit on a right-hand page.

B

MICHALENE GROSHEK
UNITED STATES

Surroundings #4

Screen printed fabric, sculpted and painted wood; 75 by 81 by 12 in. Photo: Bill Lemke.

C

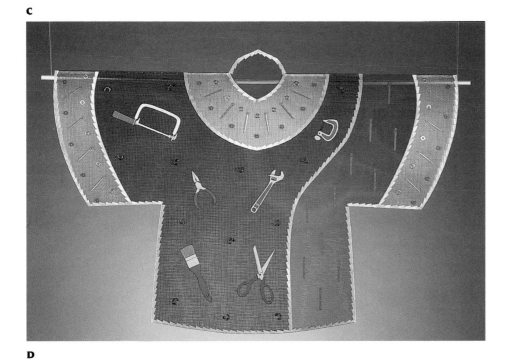

D

C

DEBRA CHASE
UNITED STATES

Handtooled Jacket

Painted aluminum screening, sheeting, and found objects; 36 by 45 by 2 in. Photo: Maje Waldo.

D

MARGRIT SCHMIDTKE
UNITED STATES

Mantle for Mankind

Appliqué, embroidery, and quilting of hand dyed and commercial cotton (mantle), coiling of painted handmade paper and felt (vessels); 96 by 84 by 96 in. Photo: BRT Photo.

A

DAVID L. POWERS
UNITED STATES

Speaker

Coiling technique with raffia, sisal, flax, and silk; 13 by 52 by 18 in.

B

OLGA DVIGOUBSKY CINNAMON
UNITED STATES

Aziza: Her power and beauty embraces me

Crochet, stuffing, and embellishment; 12 by 6 by 2 in. Photo: Jeff Owen.

I view people as being colorful, textural, and asymmetrical, resulting in a world of infinite hue and limitless diversity.

A

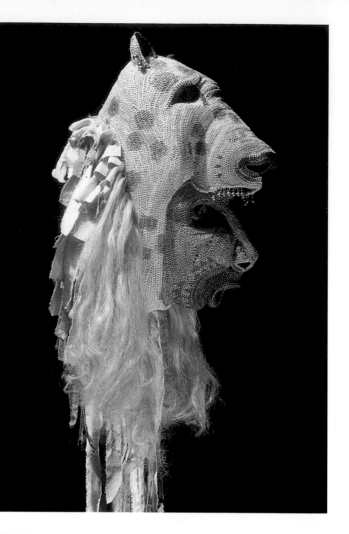

B

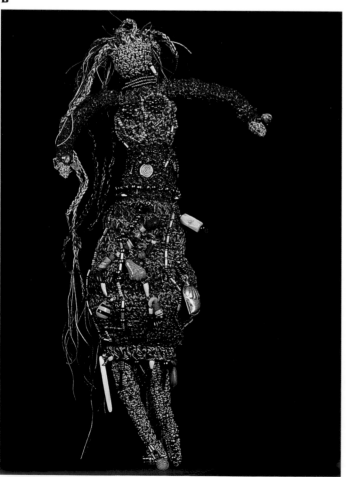

C

138

C

MIMI HOLMES
UNITED STATES

Guardians of My Heart's Desire

Constructed with paper, plaster, fiber glass, muslin, plastic pipe and embellished with beads, sequins, charms, cowrie shells, and copper wire; 60 by 72 by 60 in.

The group of figures took me nearly a year to make, and are intended to safeguard my current relationship. The gold symbolizes male energy and the silver, female.

D

ALEKSANDRA MANCZAK
POLAND

Arboretum I

Corrugated cardboard, paper tape, and flax; 40 by 200 by 14 cm. each. Photo: G. Przyborek.

This is my garden of memory. The works in this series are marked by reflection and silence.

E

MIKA WATANABE
UNITED STATES

Tranquillity

Handmade paper of kozo fiber; 15 by 13 by 15 in. each. Photo: Sibila Savage.

A

JANE INGRAM ALLEN
UNITED STATES

3 Hay Bales

Collage and painting of hand-made paper; 60 by 60 by 48 in. each. Photo: Warren Wheeler.

I live in central New York where hay bales resting in fields are a common site. These were made for installation at the Graduate Center Mall on 42nd Street in midtown Manhattan. I wanted to bring the warmth and feel of landscape to the city.

B

ITA SADAR BREZNIK
SLOVENIA

Space

Woven rayon; 400 by 350 by 350 cm. Photo: Boris Gaberseek.

The piece is hung on a flexible tube so that it can be displayed in a variety of ways.

DIVERSIONS
· · · · · · · ·

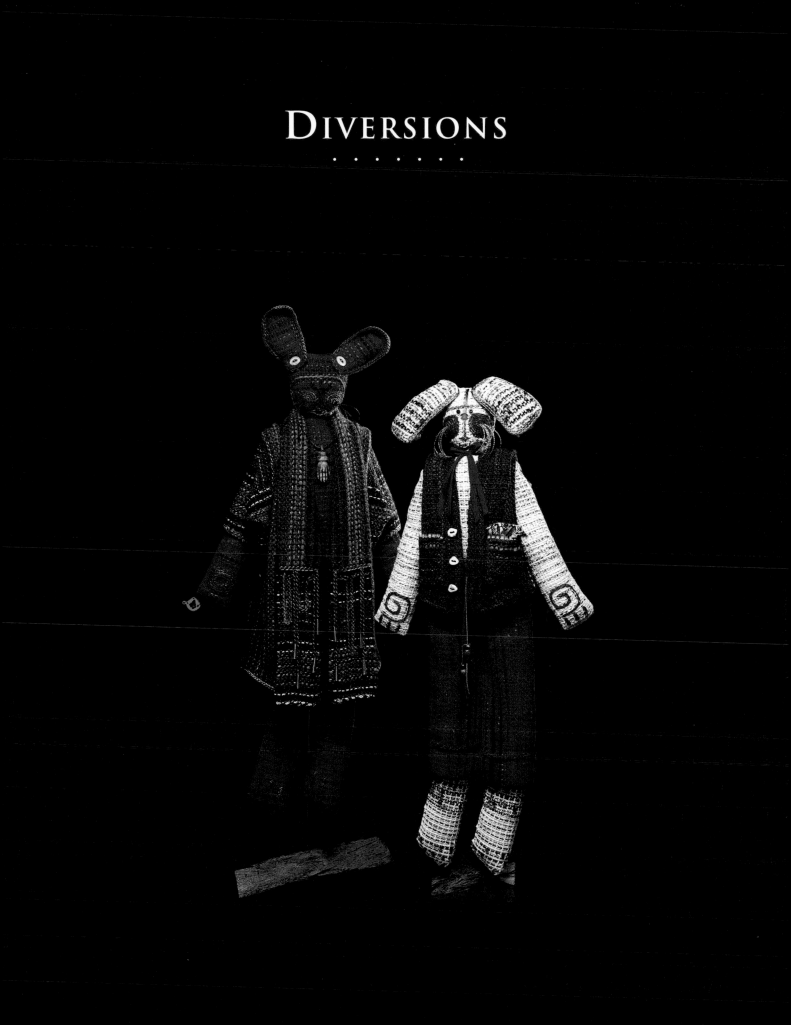

Previous Page

ALICE WATTERSON
UNITED STATES

City Rabbits

Hand weaving, crochet, stuffing, and embellishments; 30 in. high each. Photo: Gregg Mastorakis.

A

ELAINE SMALL
UNITED STATES

Fantasy

Knotted waxed linen; 6 by 11 by 3-1/2 in. Photo: Red Elf, Inc.

This is about a man "in his cups."

B

JACQUE PARSLEY
UNITED STATES

Al Restorante

Embroidery on linen, embellished with found objects; 19 by 13 by 4 in. Photo: Geoffrey Carr.

C

JENNIFFER L. ANDRZEJEWSKI
UNITED STATES

A Child's Imagination

Photo transfer, embroidery, and embellishment on cotton; 13-1/2 by 17-1/4 in.

The image is a grade school photo of my father. The headgear represents the freedom of a child's mind, where there are none of the restrictions of the adult world.

A

B

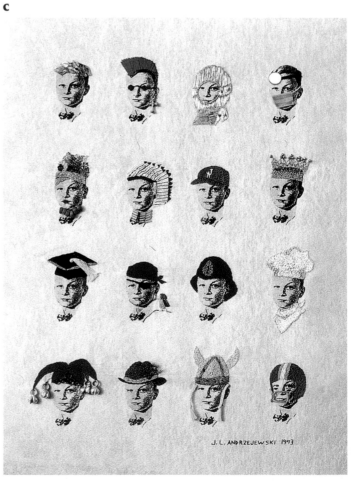

C

D

E

F

ROSITA JOHANSON
CANADA

Garden of Eden

Appliqué, machine and hand embroidery; 9-3/8 by 8-1/2 in. Photo: Lenscape Incorporated.

This is a compilation of tales my father told me when I was a child.

E

CINDY HICKOK
UNITED STATES

Hello Hello Hello Hello...

Machine embroidery; 6 by 4 in.

F

RENIE BRESKIN ADAMS
UNITED STATES

Swinging at Club Mood

Stitching, weaving, and knotless netting with cotton thread; 23-1/4 by 27-1/4 in.

I love embroidery! It allows me to work in fiber with the freedom of a painter.

A

RUTH REYNOLDS
UNITED STATES

Riva No. 2

Machine pieced, hand appliquéd commercial and dyed fabrics; 73 by 39 in.

B

KATHERINE L. MCKEARN AND DIANE MUSE
UNITED STATES

Psycho-Moms

Direct and reverse hand appliqué, machine piecing, hand quilting of commercial cotton; 61 by 55 in.

You think there's a way out, but it's really just more of the same.

C

ELLEN ANNE EDDY
UNITED STATES

Secret Garden

Machine pieced, quilted, appliquéd, and embroidered hand dyed cotton, rayon, and nylon; 54 by 50 in.

The underwater world has all the elements of a garden run wild. Even so, anemones sway as if they were sunflowers and coral grows like stalks of small hollyhocks.

D

RACHEL BRUMER
UNITED STATES

The Myth of the Individual

Hand appliqué and quilting, machine piecing, contact printing on hand dyed and commercial cotton; 63 by 51 in. Photo: Mark Frey.

My quilt studio is in the attic.

A

B

C

D

E

F

E

JILL N. PARKER-TROTTER
UNITED STATES

Red Hot Chile Peppers

Hand and machine stitching, quilting, and painting on muslin and cotton; 27-1/2 by 50 in. Photo: Izzy Howard.

This piece came about from a longing to re-visit the Southwest.

F

JUDITH VIEROW
UNITED STATES

*The Muse Dancing:
I Get a Kick Out of You*

Appliqué, piecing, machine and hand quilting of commercial fabrics; 53 by 52 in. Photo: Kevin Fitzsimons.

A

GABRIELA ORTIZ MONASTERIO
MEXICO

Doña Eduviges

Stitching and stuffing of miscellaneous fibers; 45 by 35 by 45 cm. Photo: Ricardo Dolz.

I love old people. They have their whole lives reflected in every single wrinkle.

B

LORI KEMP
UNITED STATES

Steppin' Out

Stitched and stuffed fabric, sculpted polymer clay; 22 by 20 by 7 in.

In 1991, my husband (a potter) and I retired from teaching and have concentrated on our chosen crafts.

C

DEBORAH BANYAS
UNITED STATES

Dog with Jumprope

Stitched and stuffed cotton, sculpted polymer clay; 16 by 46 by 11 in. Photo: John Seyfried.

D

DONNA PRICHARD
UNITED STATES

Morgain's Coat

Layered, sewn, distressed, and painted fabric; 52 by 56 by 2 in. Photo: Ken Wagner.

I did a series of four coats. The first was Merlin's, and the next three were Morgain's—more for my needs than hers!

A

B

C

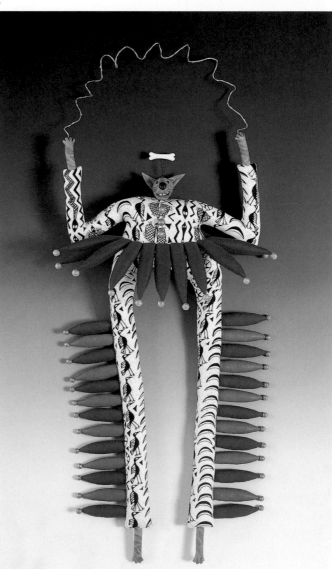

E

JOYCE MARQUESS CAREY
UNITED STATES

The Road to Agra

Machine appliqué, beading, and photo transfers on miscellaneous fabrics; 57 by 38 in.

The long bus journey to the site of the Taj Mahal was every bit as interesting as the monument itself. We saw every kind of creature and conveyance. The term, "the road to Agra," has become a code for experiences that turn out to be rewarding in unexpected ways.

F

CHRIS VIETMEIER
UNITED STATES

Sushi Trilogy: Sushi on Tap, Sunbonnet Sushi, Sushi in the Sky with Diamonds

Machine piecing, appliqué, airbrush, painting, and hand quilting of commercial fabrics; 33 by 82 in. Photo: Bill Bachuber.

This piece took several months to complete, and the entire time I was craving rice. In fact, I ate more rice then than I had in my entire life.

D

E

F

A

ALEXA ELAM
UNITED STATES .

Devil Dog

Needlewoven tapestry using cotton and linen; 3 by 3 in. each. Photo: P. Scott Minor.

B

ANNE JACKSON
ENGLAND

Reclining Nude II

Double half-hitch knotting with cotton and linen; 30 by 36 in.

Women's most visible presence in art is naked in men's paintings. Occasionally, I try to redress the balance a little.

C

ELINOR STEELE
UNITED STATES

Out There

Tapestry with wool weft and cotton warp; 48 by 46-1/2 in.

I create some of my designs on a computer. Besides being alot of fun, the technique is well suited to tapestry because of the grid-like structure of the computer image.

D

CHRISTINA BENSON VOS
UNITED STATES

Weather Vane

Tapestry using wool, rayon, cotton, and seine twine; 63 by 90 in.

E

SHEILA O'HARA
UNITED STATES

The Grass is Always Greener

Twill weaving with cotton, silk, and lurex; 22 by 31 in. Photo: Douglas Keister.

This piece was done after a friend got divorced.

F

LINDA DENIER
UNITED STATES

Oz

Gobelin tapestry with cotton warp/wool weft; 52 by 38 in.

The first time I saw The Wizard of Oz, I was so disappointed when it opened in black-and-white, but so thrilled when it turned to color.

A

B

C

D

E

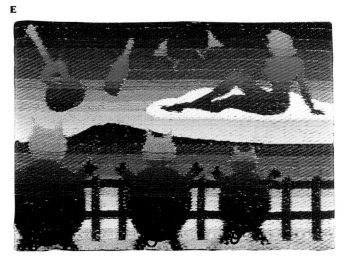

F

A

HOOP
UNITED STATES

Majestic Mosaic ('41 Packard Hearse)

Painted and applied synthetic fur.

I've had many gallery and museum shows and they are quite pleasing, but the most enjoyment I get is when I drive my fiber art around.

B

RICKI C. PUCKE
UNITED STATES

Vegetable Masks

Paper mache covered with dyed fabric and embellished with macrame and dried vegetable matter. Photo: Mel Miller.

C

HOLLY HUGHES
UNITED STATES

Roping Cowboy

Stitching, embroidery, and appliqué of miscellaneous materials; 56 by 66 by 10 in. Photo: Pat Barrett.

When I was five, I made my mom a pair of shoes from old carpet scraps and neckties. Thirty-five years later, trash is the ever-abundant material that works for me.

A

B

C

Previous Page

DORIS LOUIE
UNITED STATES

Tapestry #2, 1993

Tapestry with hand dyed wool weft yarns on linen warp; 27-1/2 by 53-1/2 in. Photo: Alan Labb.

I grew up in a large metropolitan city in the northeast United States, and now live in a small village in New Mexico. Both of these environments have been influential on my weavings.

A

MARY ZICAFOOSE
UNITED STATES

Flight into Egypt

Slit tapestry using hand dyed wool on linen warp; 45 by 63 in. Photo: Kirby Zicafoose.

B

JAY WILSON
UNITED STATES

Mandala

Flat tapestry with a linen warp and wool weft, some hand vegetal dyed; 48 by 80 in. Photo: Paul Kodama, Honolulu.

From one of the oldest sketches in my file, I found a reprieve from the complex work I had been doing. The completed design roughly parallels that of a Tees-Nos-Pos rug.

C

REBECCA BLUESTONE
UNITED STATES

New Music/7

Tapestry, embroidery, and dyeing on wool and cotton; 43 by 66 in. Photo: Herb Lotz.

This is inspired by the visual imagery of 20th-century music notation. By exploring the interaction of color, line, and fiber, I want to create a sensory experience that moves beyond the scope of the original intent of the notation.

D

ANN KEISTER
UNITED STATES

Reflections

Wool tapestry; 39 by 62 in. Photo: David Keister.

A

B

C

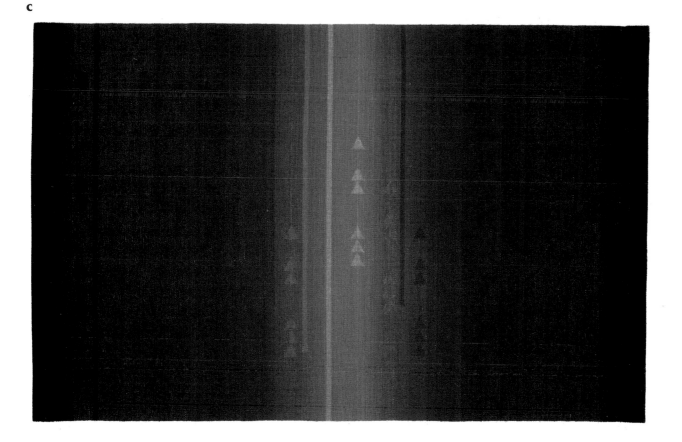

D

A

KAIJA SANELMA HARRIS
CANADA

Between August and May

6-harness weft-faced weave—2 warp systems and 2 weft systems—tapestry using cotton, wool, and silk; 170 by 148 cm. Photo: A.K. Photos, Grant A. Kernan.

I am intrigued by changing light and its influence on how we see the surrounding world. I chose wool because it absorbs light and silk because it reflects light.

B

BOJANA H. LEZNICKI
UNITED STATES

Reminiscence

Soumac tapestry using wool and silk; 62 by 47 in. Photo: Eric Guttelewitz.

C

SOYOO HYUNJOO PARK
UNITED STATES

Four Horse Power

Slit and hachure tapestry using wool, polyester, and cotton; 36 by 80 in. Photo: George Mauro.

I used an extension of the planes of light formed by the horses' musculature to create a sense of motion, and the hachure technique to emphasize this motion.

D

MARCEL MAROIS
CANADA

Like one breath in a troubled wave

High warp tapestry with wool weft and cotton warp; 108 by 105 in. Photo: Denis Chalifour.

E

SHARON MARCUS
UNITED STATES

Treasure the Dream

Tapestry using wool, cotton, linen, and goat hair; 46 by 36-1/2 in. Photo: Bill Bachhuber.

This is one of a series which investigates the possibilities of textile as "site." Artifacts, ruins, and extinct language forms are placed within a new context for reevaluation and "reading."

A

B

C

D

E

155

A

VALERIJA PURLYTE
LITHUANIA

The Willow

Tapestry with linen and wool;
100 by 70 cm.

B

LIJA RAGE
LATVIA

Women with Beast

Tapestry with wool and linen;
150 by 220 cm.

C

DONNA MARTIN
UNITED STATES

Body & Soul

Tapestry with vegetal dyed wool
and mohair; 60-1/2 by 41-1/2 in.
Photo: Hawthorne Studio.

*Prior to beginning a tapestry, I put
photos of paintings I particularly like
around the studio. This piece was
inspired by Jasper Johns' "Alley Oop."*

D

MAGDA RUBALCAVA
IRELAND

Life—Up and Down Game

Tapestry with wool weft and
cotton warp; 35 by 45 in.

*This depicts different people I've
met—the over achiever, the rainy day
person, the person who feels safe in
groups.*

E

SILVIA HEYDEN
SWITZERLAND

Tribal Dance

Exaggerated tapestry technique
using linen, wool, and cotton;
56 by 70 in. Photo: Richard
Faughn.

*It takes years to master one's instru-
ment, be it a violin or a loom; it takes
a lifetime to understand the basic
vocabulary of tapestry weaving so
that one can become free to improvise.*

A

B

C

D

E

157

A

B

A

FELIKSAS JAKUBAUSKAS
LITHUANIA

White Anxiety

Gobelin tapestry using wool and silk; 115 by 185 cm.

B

VLASTA NOVÁKOVÁ
CZECH REPUBLIC

Insight Into Microcosm

Tapestry using synthetic fiber; 250 by 180 cm. Photo: Zdenek Novák.

C

VALERIE KIRK
AUSTRALIA

Pineforest Plantation

Tapestry with wool, cotton, and linen; 90 by 140 cm.

The imagery parallels a quilt. The plantations were made to provide wood for the city, and the earth's covering is used and re-used just as a functional quilt serves its purpose.

C

D

E

D

ZILVINAS JONUTIS
LITHUANIA

Hope

Tapestry with wool, synthetics, and silk; 100 by 150 cm.

My work is based on the close union between painting and weaving.

E

MARGRIT SUTTER-FURRER
SWITZERLAND

Gruener Strom

Gobelin tapestry using wool and linen; 120 by 83 cm.

A

GEORGE-ANN BOWERS
UNITED STATES

Butte Creek

Triple-weave, warp painting, and inlay with cotton, wool, rayon, and silk; 30 by 47 by 2 in. Photo: Dana Davis.

Using multi-layer pick-up weaving allows me to transcend the limitations inherent in most loom-woven work. With this flexibility, I can bring colors and texture to the surface wherever I want and create lines and shapes which are organic, irregular, and coherent with my images.

B

BARBARA HELLER
CANADA

Stone Wall #12: Shadows

Tapestry with wool weft and linen warp; 36 by 36 in.

C

RENATA ROZSÍVALOVÁ
CZECH REPUBLIC

Meeting of the Land and the Sky

High warp tapestry of wool; 270 by 270 cm. Photo: Jaroslav Rajzik.

A

B

C

D

E

D

W H I T N E Y   J.
P E C K M A N
UNITED STATES

Sailing to Vancouver

Tapestry on Theo Moorman
threading with silk, cotton,
rayon, and wool; 60 by 42 in.
Photo: Patrick Kirby.

*I cut through, then reassembled this
piece in a collage style. The experience
of "whacking" apart a large tapestry
was very exciting. Would I create
something more dynamic or would I
end up with a bag of trash? I am
happy with the depth created by the
stacked pieces of fabric.*

E

T H E O D O R A   E L S T O N
UNITED STATES

Earth, Wind and Fire

Tapestry with wool, linen, silk,
and rayon, some spun and dyed
yarn; 37-1/2 by 46 in.

*This piece was made in an effort to
come to terms with the Oakland,
California firestorm and personal loss.*

A

IAIN YOUNG
AUSTRALIA

Shells

Flat tapestry with cotton seine twine and cotton and wool weft; 68 by 38 cm.

B

ARNOUT JONGEJAN
CANADA

The Road

Gobelin with twisted nylon warp, handspun and dyed wool weft woven on a Salish-type loom; 80 by 300 cm. Photo: Focus Photographic Services.

This is a symbolic representation of anything—organic/inorganic, material/immaterial—from its creation to its disintegration.

C

MARY LANE
UNITED STATES

Eagle Point

Tapestry using wool, linen, and cotton; 64 by 34 in.

D

JULIA MITCHELL
UNITED STATES

Siberian Iris at the Pond

Tapestry with wool and silk weft on linen warp; 60 by 36 in. Photo: Bruno Debas.

E

PAM PATRIE
UNITED STATES

Mt. Hood: Her Peak and Vale

Flat woven tapestry with cotton warp and wool weft; 60 by 36 in. Photo: Frank Engel.

This was a commission for a couple who were married at Mt. Hood.

A

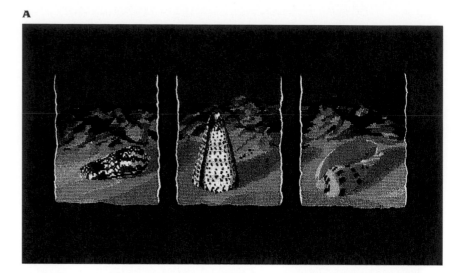

B

C

D

E

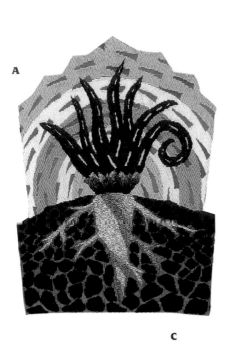

A

B

C

A

JODI JOHNSTON
UNITED STATES

Taproot

Pieced tapestry using cotton, wool, and silk; 9 by 12 in.

B

LIZA COLLINS
ENGLAND

Fecund

Tapestry with wool weft on cotton warp; 40 by 32 in.

Because I like to be spontaneous while I am weaving, I keep the process of making as direct as possible by using a simple upright scaffold frame and basic techniques and materials.

C

VICTOR JACOBY
UNITED STATES

Flowers and Mirror

Tapestry with wool weft covering cotton warp; 48 by 49 in. Photo: James D. Toms.

D

E

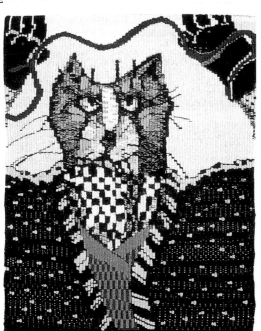

F

A

ANDRA PANDURU
ROMANIA

Verdure

Haute-lisse tapestry with wool and cotton; 140 by 90 cm.

The technique I used was inspired by tapestries of the Middle Ages, and the imagery by traditional Japanese drawing.

B

LORI JOHNSON TUREL
UNITED STATES

ShadowCast

Tapestry using horse hair, wool, silk, jute, and cotton; 86 by 64 in. Photo: Bill Bachhuber.

C

ANNA BUCZKOWSKA
POLAND

Collection II

Gobelin tapestry using wool, flax, and synthetic fibers; 250 by 160 cm.

Working in textiles makes it possible to obtain a multiplicity of forms— from flat, painterly planes to complicated structures.

D

ZINAIDA VOGELIENE
LITHUANIA

Black Summer I

Tapestry with wool, silk, and flax; 260 by 260 cm. Photo: A. Sidorenko.

E

DEANN RUBIN
UNITED STATES

Cat with Fiber

Tapestry with cotton and embroidery thread; 6 by 8 in. Photo: Splash Studios.

The image deals with the fears of crime individuals have in today's society.

F

LETITIA KAMINSKI ROLLER
UNITED STATES

Scherzo

Wool tapestry; 10 by 10 in.

A

B

C

A

JANET AUSTIN
UNITED STATES

Self Portrait (Purple Sketch)
Tapestry with cotton warp and
wool weft; 17 by 17 in.

B

LOIS KENNEDY-PAINE
CANADA

Reclining Woman
Gobelin tapestry with wool weft
and cotton warp; 18 by 12 in.
Photo: Grant Kernan, AK Photos.

D

E

C

MARILYN REA-
MENZIES
NEW ZEALAND

Portrait of a Man

Tapestry with wool and cotton
weft and cotton warp; 142 by 87
cm.

D

RUTH MANNING
UNITED STATES

Trio in a Major Diner

Tapestry with wool and cotton
seine twine; 78 by 26 in. Photo:
Richard Margolis.

E

ULRIKA LEANDER
UNITED STATES

The Family Portrait

Soumac tapestry with cotton
warp and wool weft; 46 by 56 in.
Photo: J. Nave.

*I take enormous care and pride in cre-
ating a tapestry that is just right for
my client. Perfect craftsmanship and
using high quality materials were
ideals instilled in me during years of
training in my native country,
Sweden.*

A

SUZANNE PRETTY
UNITED STATES

Wash Days

Tapestry with wool, silk, and cotton on a linen warp; 53 by 42 in.

B

ALEXANDRA S. FRIEDMAN
UNITED STATES

Three Graces

Modified gobelin tapestry with wool and cotton; 50 by 59 in.

C

AUDREY MOORE
UNITED STATES

Earth Wrapping

Wool tapestry using Navajo loom; 46 by 38 in. Photo: Jerome Hart.

D

SHEILA O'HARA
UNITED STATES

If Artists Had Nine Lives

Four warp twill weaving with cotton, silk, and lurex; 22 by 32 in. Photo: Douglas Keister.

Van Gogh and Magritte cruise down the highway in a Rolls Royce under a sky dotted with Magritte's apples and Van Gogh's spinning stars.

E

TERESA GRAHAM SALT
UNITED STATES

Wild Ride

Tapestry with silk twist; 10 by 11 in.

A

B

C

D

E

A

A

TOMMYE MCCLURE SCANLIN
UNITED STATES

Crow-Dark Angel…

Wool and cotton tapestry; 52 by 52 in. Photo: Hank Margeson.

B

MARGO MACDONALD
UNITED STATES

You Have Only Waited for This Moment to Arrive

Tapestry with cotton warp and wool weft; 36 by 30 in.

This was inspired by the Balkan secession from the Soviet Union. The blackbird, common to these regions, takes a piece of the Soviet flag to build its nest. The title refers to the old Beatles song, which also inspired me with its message of freedom.

C

ELINOR STEELE
UNITED STATES

Winter Windows

Variation of Gobelin tapestry with wool and rayon on cotton warp; 63 by 26 in.

This design was inspired by the plants in my bedroom window and the dancing lights and shadows caused by cars passing at night.

D

IRINA ALOVA
RUSSIA

Another World

Wool tapestry; 160 by 246 cm.

E

AINA MUZE
LATVIA

Night

Tapestry with wool and linen; 100 by 100 cm.

B

C

D

E

A

JUDY CHICAGO AND AUDREY COWAN
UNITED STATES

The Fall

Modified Aubusson with crewel wool and dyed silk; 18 by 4-1/2 ft. Photo: Donald Woodman. Design: J. Chicago; weaving: A. Cowan.

This is part of "The Holocaust Project: From Darkness Into Light."

B

INGE NORGAARD
UNITED STATES

The Messengers

Free style Gobelin tapestry using cotton and wool; 50 by 78 in. Photo: C. Haniford

C

RAMONA SAKIEWSTEWA
UNITED STATES

Spotted Corn

Wool tapestry using Pueblo and Navajo techniques; 96 by 49 in. Photo: H. Lotz.

This is an abstraction of the different types and colors of corn grown by the Hopi people.

D

SUSAN IVERSON
UNITED STATES

Night View - Focus

Tapestry with wool on linen warp; 90 by 36 in. Photo: Katherine Wetzel.

This is part of a series that is about viewing landscape and architecture at different times of the day. I am concerned with the colors and forms that we see, or think we see, in low-light situations.

A

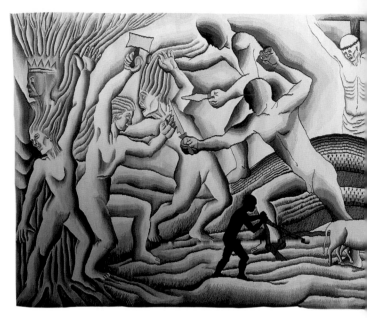

B

C

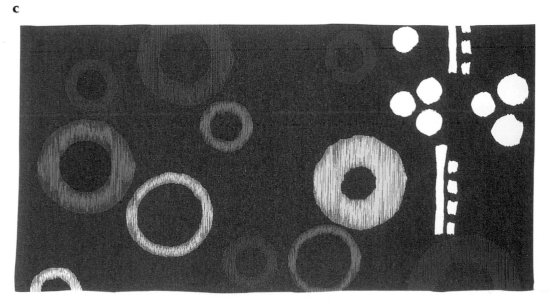

D

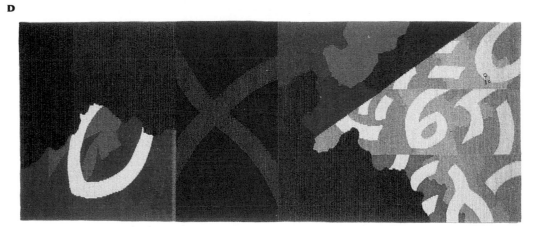

A

ANDREW SCHNEIDER
UKRAINE

Europe

Wool and cotton tapestry; 100 by 180 cm.

B

YURI SCHNEIDER
UKRAINE

The Tree of Life

Wool tapestry; 200 by 145 cm.

C

SARA HOTCHKISS
UNITED STATES

Tree of Life

Tapestry using cotton, 48 by 72 in. Photo: Dennis Griggs.

C

B

D

JANET MOORE
UNITED STATES

It's Not Easy...

Shaped tapestry with wool and cotton; 89 by 72 in. Photo: Gary Hunt.

E

SHEILA HELD
UNITED STATES

The Old Order of the Sun

Interlocked weft tapestry with wool, silk, cotton, and metallic yarns; 50 by 50 in. Photo: Dave Altman.

Though the images in my work take precedence over the techniques, I find the medium of weaving an appropriate metaphor for the structure of reality: the vertical warp threads symbolize that which is permanent and absolute; the weft threads symbolize that which is pliant and ever-changing.

F

MARY F. DONOVAN
UNITED STATES

When the Harbinger from the East Finally Arrived Out West, She Realized She Had the Wrong Address

Slit tapestry with wool, linen, cotton, and synthetic yarn; 56 by 68 in.

Whether I work in an abstract or narrative style, my intent is to depict a response to the social/cultural relationships in my life.

E

F

A

KRISTIN CARLSEN ROWLEY
COLOMBIA

The Dream of Roberto

Tapestry using embroidery floss; 9 by 8 by 5-1/2 in.

Roberto is an architect, a lover, and a dreamer.

B

BIRGITTA LJUNGBERG
SWEDEN

Sehem

Tapestry with flax, cotton, gold lamé, and neon; 60 by 60 by 60 by 56 cm. Photo: Bosse Ljungberg.

Sehem was the Egyptian god representing life energy.

C

SANDY ADAIR
UNITED STATES

Arboretum Screen II

Tapestry with embroidery overlay using wool, cotton, and silk; 66 by 66 in. Photo: John Scarlotta.

The landscape, with its ever changing colors and moods, has been a continual source of inspiration for my work.

D

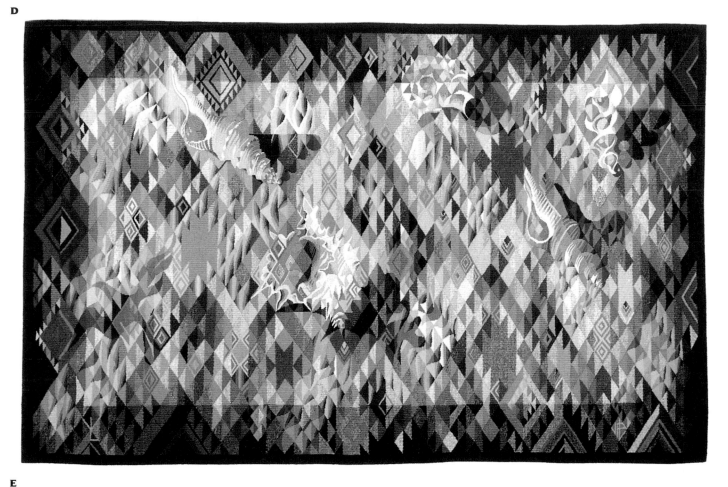

E

D

YAEL LURIE AND
JEAN PIERRE
LAROCHETTE
UNITED STATES

Spirals

Aubusson and other tapestry
techniques with cotton warp
and wool, linen, silk, and cotton
weft; 61 by 39 in. Photo: Michel
Irwin.

E

MARIA LUISA
FERREIRA
PORTUGAL

Poppies

High warp tapestry with linen,
cotton, and silk; 160 by 165 cm.
Photo: Jose Miguel Figueiredo.

A

JOAN GRIFFIN
UNITED STATES

Fallen Image

Tapestry with wool/silk weft and cotton warp; 57 by 43 by 2 in.

B

CRISTINA FERRER
ARGENTINA

Sin Hogar

Tapestry with linen and wool; 180 by 120 cm. Photo: Gustavo Alemany.

C

CECILIA BLOMBERG
UNITED STATES

The Guardian of the Gazebo

Tapestry with wool weft and cotton seine twine warp; 60 by 39 in.

A

B

C

D

P E T E R H A R R I S
CANADA

Nightmare

Flat woven wool tapestry on a linen warp; 36 by 48 in.

More than once people have told me that they assumed the weaver to be a woman. I thought it was just my private phobia.

E

**E L I Z A B E T H J.
B U C K L E Y**
UNITED STATES

Desert Flight

Aubusson tapestry with wool and cotton; 21-3/8 by 16-1/2 in.

The idea for this piece began with a piece of driftwood shaped like a bird in flight. As I sketched and studied it, I thought of the 93-year-old woman who gave me the driftwood from her collection of weathered bones, shells, and rocks. As she approached death, she repeatedly wrote of the spirit preparing for flight.

D

E

A

KATHLEEN MOLLOHAN
UNITED STATES

Yellowstone Rebirth #2

Four-harness wool tapestry in undulating twill; 48 by 34 in. Photo: Craig Sharpe.

The subject is the devastating Yellowstone Park forest fire. It is one of a series on the theme of new life arising out of destruction.

B

NINA LAPTCHIK
UKRAINE

Us and Them

Tapestry with wool, cotton, and silk; 170 by 200 cm. Photo: Gleb Vysheslavski.

People should never forget that we do not exist in isolation—we are all together.

C

SOYOO HYUNJOO PARK
UNITED STATES

Human Race

Hachure, slit, and pick and pick tapestry with cotton, wool, polyester, and silk; 120 by 48 in. Photo: George Mauro.

D

CATHERINE HOFFMANN
AUSTRALIA

The Gymnasts

Flat woven tapestry with wool, silk, linen, gold fabric strips on a cotton seine twine warp; 106 by 185 cm. Photo: Kevin Carvalho.

I meant to capture forever a fleeting moment in the lives of two young gymnasts. It is a celebration of their vigor and youthful talent.

E

BETTY HILTON-NASH
UNITED STATES

Mojock

Flat tapestry with wool weft and cotton warp; 39 by 30 in. Photo: Trevor Nash.

A

B

C

D

E

A

C RESSIDE C OLLETTE
AUSTRALIA

Of the Spirit and the Flesh

Tapestry with cotton warp and
wool, cotton, and rayon weft;
146 by 113 cm. Photo: Tim
Gresham.

*My particular interest has been to
interpret, in woven form, the quality
of the drawn line in all its gestures—
from direct and vigorous to soft and
delicate.*

B

L U R ULAI
CHINA

Organ

Interlacing technique using
jute, wool, and silk; 180 by 200
by 10 cm.

C

F IONA R.
H UTCHISON
SCOTLAND

Transis Ample Tai

Tapestry with wool, cotton, and
linen weft and mohair warp; 120
by 60 in. Photo: David Kinney;
collection of Perth Royal
Infirmary.

*My work is influenced by my love of
the sea and sailing.*

A

B

C

D

**TIM GRESHAM
AND ROBYN
MOUNTCASTLE**
AUSTRALIA

The Garden of Infinite Desires

Gobelin tapestry with wool and
cotton; 245 by 215 cm.

*This work was collaboratively
designed and woven by us and other
members of "The Tapestry Weavers."*

E

JENNY HANSEN
DENMARK

The Red Gate

Slit tapestry using cotton; 200
by 180 cm.

F

**MINA LEVITAN-
BABENSKIENE**
LITHUANIA

The Birth of the Stone

Tapestry using wool, flax, and
silk; 170 by 100 cm.

D

E

F

A

MARIE SCHNEIDER-
SENIUK
UKRAINE

Landscape With Lake
Wool tapestry; 180 by 250 cm.

B

SERGEY MINAEV
RUSSIA

Daydream I
Tapestry using wool, synthetic
fibers, and flax; 101 by 101 cm.
Photo: V. Antoshenkov.

C

ANATOLY RUBTZOV
RUSSIA

Morning
Wool tapestry; 100 by 100 cm.

A

B

C

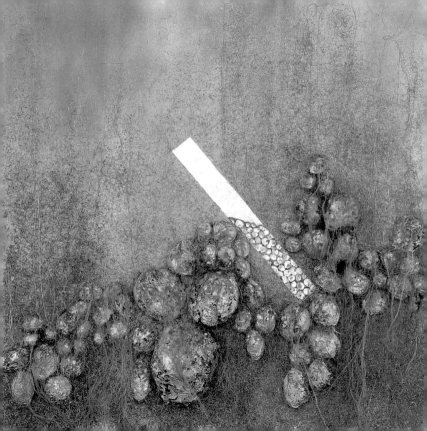

A

Previous Page

Previous Page

YAEL BENTOVIM
UNITED STATES

Rock Series #3

Paper molding, shredded fiber collage, and painting; 36 by 36 in. Photo: Claire Curran.

A

CAROLYN PRINCE
BATCHELOR
UNITED STATES

Firebird

Painted, rolled, braided, knotted, and sewn paper; 23 by 48 by 1 in. Photo: Dee Cole.

My paper garments are nonwearable models of idealized clothing. These symbolic garments are important to me, both as sculptures seen as discrete shapes and as surfaces for embellishment which sometimes imitates fabric structures.

B

GLORIA ZMOLEK
SMITH
UNITED STATES

Only a Thousand Lives: Syria, Turkey, Afghanistan

Handmade paper using kozo, abaca, and flax with stenciling and pulp painting techniques; 42 by 15 by 3 in.

This project was started in response to the threat of war in the Persian Gulf, and is an expression of my feelings about war in general.

B

C

IRENE MAGINNIS
UNITED STATES

Temple Series: Centering

Painting of poured cotton pulps and strip piecing; 43 by 30 in. Photo: Jeff Sprang.

C

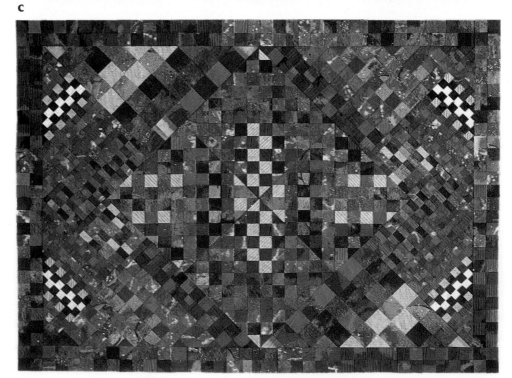

D

LOIS JAMES
UNITED STATES

Home Fronts

Papermaking, photo silkscreen, and collage using flax, kozo, and Japanese stencil papers; 16 by 66 in. Photo: Victoria Damrel.

The repetitive action of making paper becomes a ritual experience with ties to cultures in which paper is used in ritual.

D

E

F

E

BARBARA P. FAST
UNITED STATES

Playing on the Grid

Cast and painted abaca; 52 by 37 by 4 in.

The tradition of quilting among Mennonite women in my family has been an important influence on my work.

F

MARJORIE HOELTZEL
UNITED STATES

Grand Canyon

Machine stitchery on hand-made paper and miscellaneous fabrics; 35 by 19 in.

I wanted to depict the spiritual and emotional impact of being at the Grand Canyon. It was a humbling experience, rather like being in 10,000 cathedrals.

A

T RACY K RUMM
U NITED S TATES

Her Sorrow, Unmasked

Woven paper embedded in cast cotton and abaca, then surface embellished with oil and chalk pastels and crocheted wire; 36 by 39 in. Photo: Courtesy Hibberd-McGrath Gallery, Breckenridge, Colorado.

B

S OPHIE A CHESON
U NITED S TATES

Origins

Embossing, drawing, sewing, and collage of cotton fiber handmade paper; 27 by 32 in.

My work is landscape oriented and mirrors what I experience in my travels. I am influenced by medieval art.

C

B ETSY R. M IRAGLIA
U NITED S TATES

Empty Nest

Free cast, manipulated pigment-colored pulp and acrylic stenciling; 40 by 48 in.

D

M ONA W ATERHOUSE
U NITED S TATES

Ancient Writings: Setting Boundaries

Paper forming with abaca and cotton fibers, applying dyes in layers; 35 by 38 in.

A

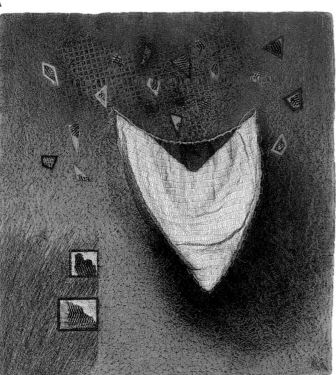

B

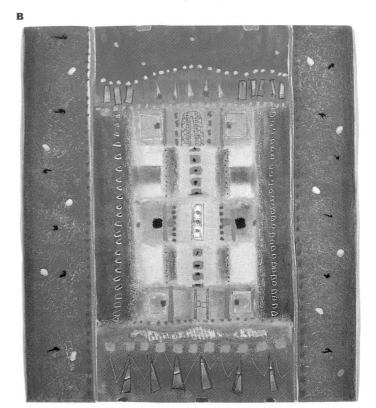

C

E

BARBARA SIEDLECKA
ENGLAND

Guardians of the Fresco

Recycled materials floated in paper pulp and enhanced with pigments; 45 by 32 cm.

This is one of a series resulting from the study of rock chapels of Anatolia.

F

MARJORIE TOMCHUK
UNITED STATES

Another Channel

Cast, stenciled, airbrushed, and painted handmade paper; 40 by 32 in.

G

NANCY PRICHARD
UNITED STATES

Sacred Cow

Paper casting, collage, and machine stitching using hand-made and found papers, fabric, and electrostatic transparencies; 19 by 22 in. Photo: Bruce Prichard.

This is from my series, "Icons For Our Times," which deals with the cyclical effects of greed and how man has interfered with the natural harmony and balance of creation.

D

E

F

G

A

B

C

D

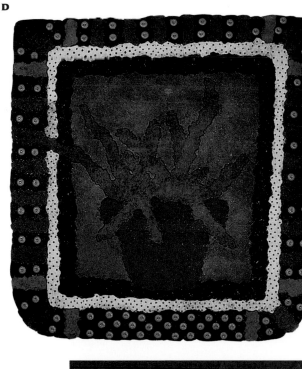

E

A

LYN PIERRE
UNITED STATES

The Odyssey

Dyed and pigmented handmade paper; 41 by 32 in. Photo: Red Elf, St. Louis.

My first love was printmaking, but I have found new freedom in image making by working with paper as a medium.

B

SHARON PHIPPS KUMP
UNITED STATES

The Other Side

Dyed and cast handmade paper, collage, drawing, stenciling, sewing, and stamping; 70 by 57 in.

The detail that I incorporate into my work gives me time to pursue the essence of the piece—the emotion, thought, or experience that precipitates the process.

C

PAI GENIENAAR-TORLEY
THE NETHERLANDS

No Sense of Time

Pulp painting on handmade paper made with linen, sisal, silk, flax, cotton, and straw cellulose; 100 by 130 cm.

Grapevines in the Fall inspired this piece in which I attempted to capture the spirit of the vine in the fiber.

D

CLAUDIA LEE
UNITED STATES

Buttons and Aloe

Hand formed, painted, and embellished pulp; 25 by 26 in. Photo: Joe Muncey.

E

NICOLE DEXTRAS
CANADA

Miss Congeniality

Handmade paper, photo transfer, and dyes on foam core; 60 by 72 by 48 in.

My interest in photography goes back to high school, but it wasn't until I discovered liquid emulsions and transfers that I began to incorporate photo images into my art. I feel that the use of the photograph with handmade paper creates a fertile ground of paradoxes to address complex issues.

A

S U S A N L E O P O L D
CANADA

Childhood Memories

Handmade paper and collage
using post-consumer materials;
8 by 10 in. Photo: See Spot Run.

B

E V A G A L L A N T
UNITED STATES

Segesta Souvenirs

Cast handmade paper using
flax; 16 by 11 by 7 in. Photo:
Katherine Rose.

*There is an inherent spiritual quality
to handmade paper. Its subtle yet
strong presence often suggests both a
concept and a solution.*

A

B

C

J A N E D U N N E W O L D
UNITED STATES

The Girl's Guide to Life

Painted, stamped, and stitched
handmade paper using silk,
photo copy transfers, and gold
leaf; 12 by 12 by 2 in.

*This is an original book and text pro-
duced in limited, entirely handmade
editions. Some of the other texts:
"always use sunscreen," "date nice
boys," "juggle it all like superwoman,"
and "only cook if you want to."*

C

D

CLARE ARENDS
ENGLAND

Votive

Paper made with cotton linters tied with linen yarn; 10 by 10 by 13 in. Photo: Rufford Craft Centre, Nottinghamshire.

A unit can be made from many parts, but each is necessary for the whole to function.

E

RAIJA JOKINEN
FINLAND

From the Orbit

Handmade and painted paper and paper yarn; 160 by 160 by 5 cm.

I have always been interested in a graphic means of expression, but instead of drawing lines on paper, I draw with paper. This piece expresses the fragile union of particles—fusion is as likely as decomposition.

F

CAS HOLMES
ENGLAND

Spiral

Handmade, dyed, layered, and stitched paper; 160 cm. diameter. Photo: John Ware.

This was made at a time I was "going around in circles."

D

E

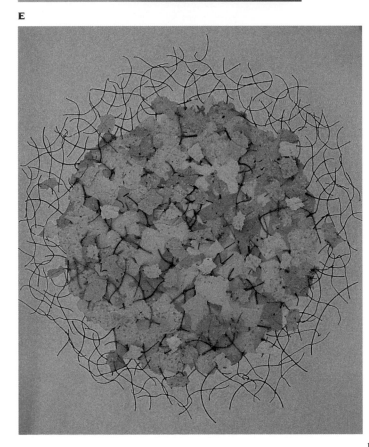

F

A

ANJA GARTZKE
GERMANY

Experimental Felt

Double woven and steamed wool and polyester; 24 by 28 cm.

During the weaving this construction is totally flat, but in the finishing process, it becomes almost three dimensional because of the natural ability of wool to felt and shrink.

B

CHAD ALICE HAGEN
UNITED STATES

Palace Walk

Hand felting, shibori, and stitched construction; 64 by 85 in. Photo: Gerald Sedgewich.

Felt is an incredible substance with which to work; it has extraordinary capacities to absorb color, light, and sound. I want to construct enormous walls from small fragments—moveable textile walls that could create a space of quiet, for reflection and thought.

C

KAREN S. PAGE
UNITED STATES

Stratum No. 5

Hand felted and cut wool; 46 by 56 in. Photo: Clifton Page.

The technique of cutting away the surface reveals the underlying structure as it creates a new configuration of marks on the surface.

D

MITSUKO TARUI
JAPAN

Birthstone III

Hand felted and dyed wool and silk; 30 by 55 in. Photo: Stephen Brayne.

Even though felting is a very old technique, I believe it has many possibilities to be used in new ways to make fiber art that is very contemporary.

E

MARIA J. STACHOWSKA
ENGLAND

Folk Memories

Hand felted and dyed wool and silk; 101 by 74 cm. Photo: Andrew Yale.

Light and color captivate me, so I especially enjoy feltmaking because of the ease with which I can apply color to the fabric.

A

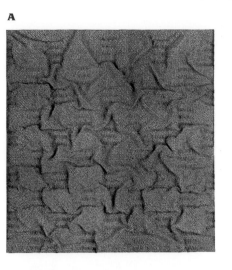

B

C

D

E

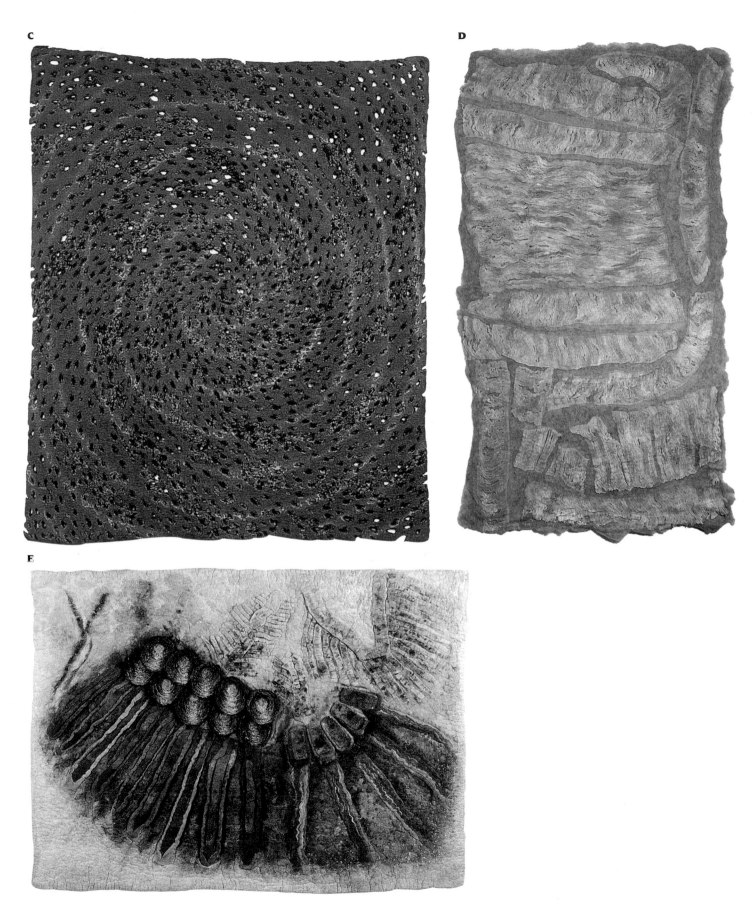

A

MOLLY R.M.
FOWLER
UNITED STATES

Bali/Attraction Tourist

Felting, silk papermaking, knotless netting, and needlework;
68 by 36 by 7 in. Collection of
Mr. and Mrs. R. Michael Curran.

*This is a composite of a trip the Currans
took to this idyllic tropical island.*

B

MICHELE G. WOOD
UNITED STATES

Corridor

Felting, dyeing cutting and
piecing; 25 by 30 in. Photo:
Naomi Towner.

C

MARIA ASSUNTA
FORSTER FERRUGEM
BRAZIL

**In Honor of the Art Museum of
Rio Grande do Sul State**

Handmade, embroidered felt;
100 by 100 cm.

*The idea for this piece came from the
ionic columns, stained glass windows,
and other architectural elements of the
museum.*

B

C

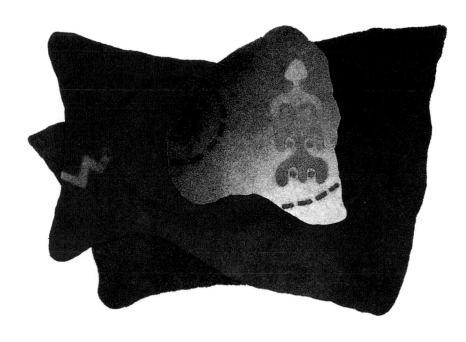

D

PATRICIA H. SPARK
UNITED STATES

Legacy Series, The 1st Mother & Her Daughters: Past, Present, Future

Hand felting, piecing, and dyeing; 36 by 48 in.

This series is the result of 20 years of research into the folk motifs of Central Asia.

E

LINDA LAINO
UNITED STATES

Vestigial Parts

Felting, embroidery, and painting; 40 by 60 by 4 in.

F

LINDA LIVESEY
ENGLAND

The Three Ladies

Painted and embroidered handmade felt; 19 by 19 in. Photo: G. Templeton.

This was inspired by French head-dresses and is one of a series I did on this subject.

F

A

KAREN STAHLECKER
UNITED STATES

Winter Gothic

Asian papermaking techniques using kozo fiber and linen, personal casting and assembly; 108 by 135 by 18 in.

The winters in Anchorage, Alaska where I live are very long. This was conceived partly in response to those winters and partly in response to needing smaller works on hand for exhibition.

B

JOAN HALL
UNITED STATES

Forsythe

Handmade paper and mixed media printing; 108 by 72 in. Photo: Hal Bundy.

While my fragmented images and layered abstractions are devoid of people, they are very much about human nature.

Previous Page

KATHLEEN SHARP
UNITED STATES

Summer House Triptych

Hand and machine pieced, appliquéd, and quilted cotton and cotton/rayon; 86 by 61 in. Photo: John Brennan.

A

GERRY CHASE
UNITED STATES

Nine-Patch I: Vessels

Pieced, appliquéd, and quilted cotton and metallic fabrics; 29 by 29 in. Photo: Roger Schreiber; collection of Meg Singer, Seattle, Washington.

I work intuitively, approaching each piece as if, even while still formless, it possesses some degree of coalescence, and my job is to discover how it intends to express itself.

B

SUZAN FRIEDLAND
UNITED STATES

Anasazi

Hand painted and machine quilted cotton; 83 by 73 in. Photo: Sharon Risedorph.

A Navajo guide took me on a tour of Canyon de Chelly; the Anasazi art and ruins made a lasting impression.

C

MARIE-JOSÉ DANZON
CANADA

Blind Memories

Log Cabin piecing and appliqué using upholstery and drapery fabric; 40 by 64 in. Photo: See Spot Run, Toronto.

D

LYNNE HELLER
CANADA

Mola/Quilt #27

Reverse appliqué and couching of wool, silk, cotton, and lame; 56 by 33 by 1 in. Photo: A. Guacci.

The tactile pleasure of manipulating fabric has encouraged me to use traditional techniques to create contemporary work.

A

B

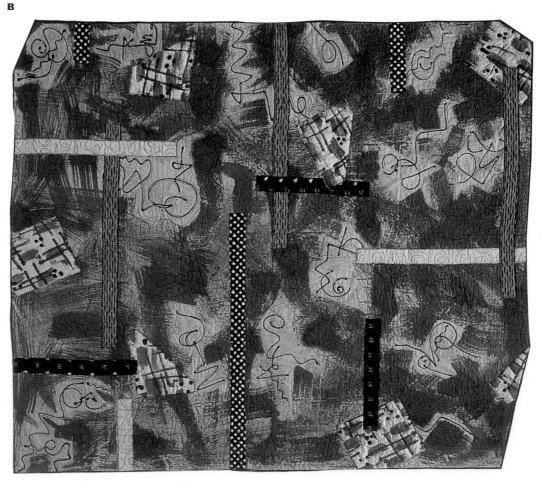

C

D

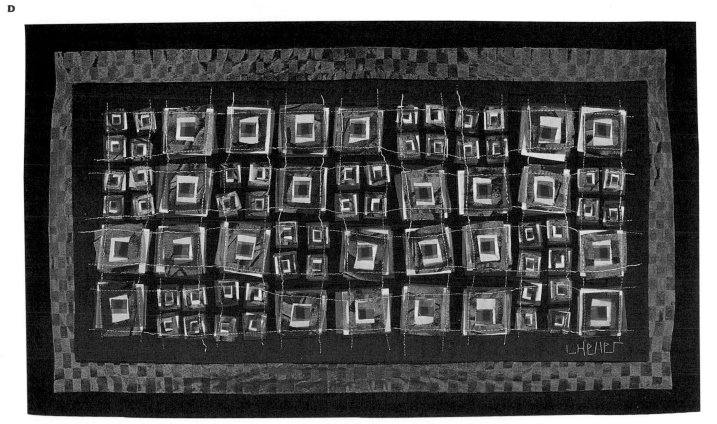

A

ANN M. ADAMS
UNITED STATES

Radiant Energy

Dyed by direct application, wax resist block printed, and machine quilted cotton; 50 by 59 in.

This is from a series celebrating spirituality, sensuality, art, food, friendship, and children.

B

JUDY BECKER
UNITED STATES

Homage: Clay

Machine pieced and quilted taffeta, satin, silk, drapery fabric, and cotton; 57 by 47 in. Photo: David Caras.

The piece is a Valentine for Fred: husband, lawyer, potter, and ever-interesting man.

C

SUSAN WEBB LEE
UNITED STATES

Longing to Lose Control

Machine quilted, appliquéd, and embroidered cotton; 48 by 49-1/2 in. Photo: Pat Staub.

D

PAULA K. FORESMAN
UNITED STATES

Hubcaps II: Color Wheel

Machine piecing, hand quilting, silkscreening on cotton; 42 by 38 in.

E

GERI KINNEAR
UNITED STATES

Letting Go

Machine appliquéd and quilted cotton; 44 by 44 in.

When I retired from teaching in 1993, I found it difficult to "let go."

F

SUZANNE EVENSON
UNITED STATES

In the Garden of My Mother's Dreams

Machine pieced and quilted cotton, embellished with beads; 40 by 40 in. Photo: Chas Krider.

A

B

C

D

E

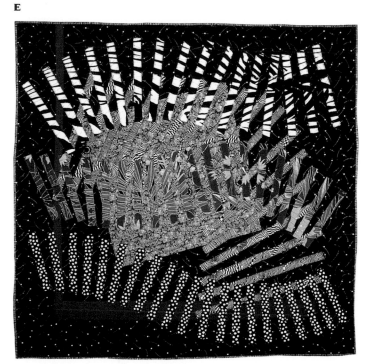

F

207

A

**B A R B A R A   L Y D E C K E R
C R A N E**
U N I T E D   S T A T E S

Inuit Map

Machine pieced, hand and
machine quilted hand painted
cotton; 53 by 72 in. Photo:
David Caras.

B

**M E I N Y   V E R M A A S -
V A N   D E R   H E I D E**
U N I T E D   S T A T E S

*Earth Quilt #27: Fields of Color
IX*

Machine pieced and quilted
cotton; 82 by 48 in.

*Dutch painters Piet Mondriaan and
Vincent van Gogh, as well as tulips
and other flowers of Holland inspire
my work. In this series, various
aspects of simultaneous contrast are
used to create optical illusions.*

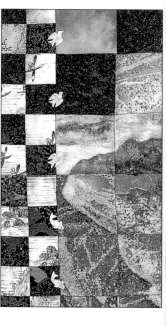

A

B

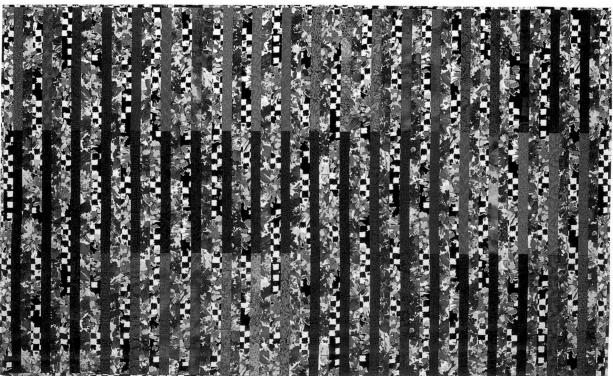

C

D

C

ANNE DE LA MAUVINIERE SILVA
CANADA

Fantasia

Machine pieced and hand quilted cotton and cotton/silk blend; 57 by 57 in. Photo: M. Bowie.

D

NANCY CRASCO
UNITED STATES

Gyre and Gimbel

Machine pieced and hand appliquéd and quilted commercial and hand painted fabrics; 94 by 61 in. Photo: David Caras.

The five major gyres of the ocean act as whirlpools, pulling plastic refuse and other flotsam near to their centers.

A

CAMILLE REMME
CANADA

Celtic Quest

Machine stitched dyed and
commercial cotton; 58 by 72 in.

*I have authored five quilt books, and
Celtic lore is my new interest.*

B

KRISTINA BECKER
UNITED STATES

Four Black Birds

Hand appliquéd and quilted
cotton; 61 by 61 in. Photo:
Sharon Risedorph.

*I love the bright colors in
Pennsylvania Dutch quilts, but I
wanted mine to be different so I used
the yellow as a "neutral" background.*

C

RUTH GARRISON
UNITED STATES

Tossing and Turning 3: Contained

Machine pieced and quilted
dye-painted cotton; 40 by 40 in.

D

PAULA J. SARGE
UNITED STATES

Rocky Road

Machine pieced and quilted
cotton; 42 by 38 in. Photo:
Camille Gerace.

E

NANCY SMITH
UNITED STATES

Star Flight

Machine pieced and appliquéd,
hand quilted cotton and lame;
54 by 62 in.

A

B

C

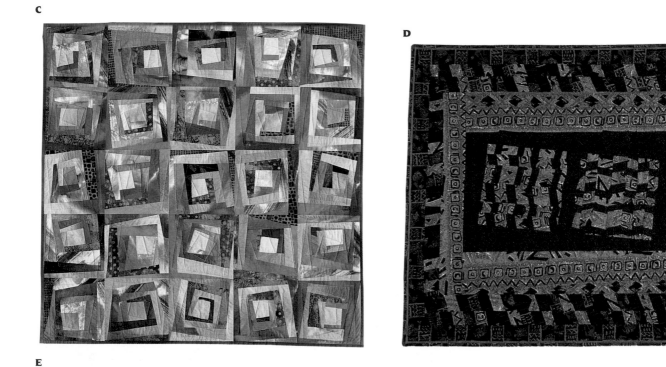

D

E

A

B

C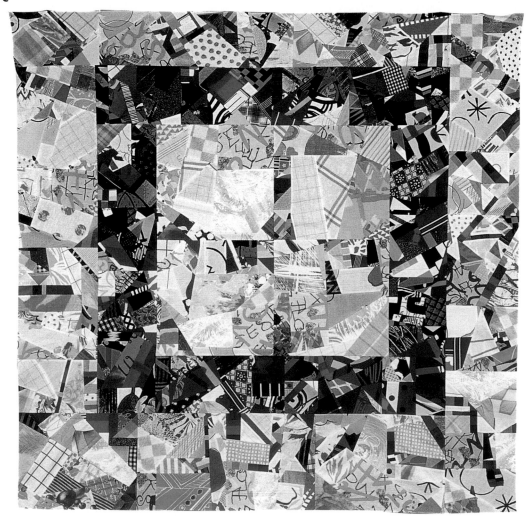

A

CHERILYN MARTIN
THE NETHERLANDS

Walls

Machine quilting and embroidery on hand painted silk, cotton, and synthetics; 45 by 60 cm.

B

ALISON SCHWABE
AUSTRALIA

Western Desert © 1993

Machine pieced, quilted, and airbrushed cotton and cotton blends; 30 by 30 in. Photo: John Bonath, Mad Dog Studio.

This is part of my "Colour Memory" series.

C

SYLVIA H. EINSTEIN
UNITED STATES

Grenzen

Machine pieced and quilted cotton and cotton blends; 59 by 60 in. Photo: David Caras.

The title translates into "borders" or "boundaries."

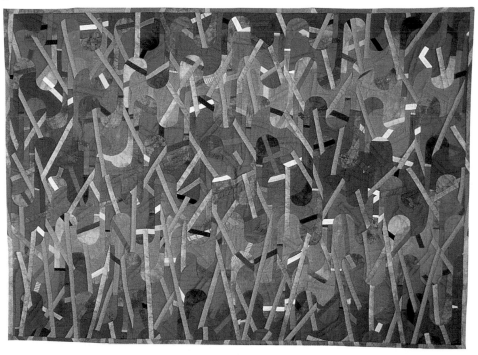

FIONA GAVENS
AUSTRALIA

Bush Fragments IV-Regrowth

Machine pieced and quilted mixed fabrics; 122 by 87 cm. Photo: Geoff Crispin.

The paddock looks "empty" from a distance, but up close a myriad of details are revealed.

E

DORLE STERN-STRAETER
GERMANY

No Exit

Crazy quilt technique using cotton and silk; 64 by 65 in. Photo: Patricia Fliegauf.

E

A

J A N E   B U R C H
C O C H R A N
U N I T E D   S T A T E S

Inner Sanctum

Appliquéd using beads,
machine pieced commercial
fabric, and found objects; 37 by
45 in. Photo: Pam Monfort.

B

P A T T Y   H A W K I N S
U N I T E D   S T A T E S

Grand Canyon Vista © 1992

Randon checkerboard strip
piecing and inlay construction
of hand dyed and commercial
cottons; 92 by 83 in. Photo: Ken
Sanville.

C

J U D I T H   T R A G E R
United States

*Who Are These Children Dressed
in Red?*

Machine pieced and hand quilted cotton; 60 by 47 in. Photo:
Ken Sanville.

*I am doing a narrative series docu-
menting the heritage of my family.
This alludes to the Underground
Railroad.*

D

M I C H A E L   A .
C U M M I N G S
U N I T E D   S T A T E S

Take My Brother Home

Appliquéd cotton, satin, African
fabrics, hand dyed cotton, and
photo transfer; 60 by 60 in.
Photo: Sara Wells.

*The male form on the cross represents
the unjust suffering of our black
brothers.*

E

J E A N N E   L Y O N S
B U T L E R
U N I T E D   S T A T E S

Dance of Joy © 1993

Hand appliquéd and machine
quilted cotton; 66-3/4 by 71-1/2
in. Photo: Karen Bell.

*The quilt speaks to the bonds that are
uplifting.*

A

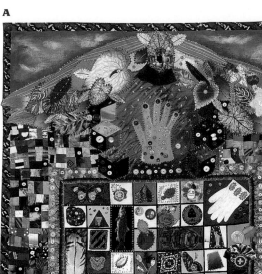

B

C

D

E

215

A

VIRGINIA J. SCHLOSSER
UNITED STATES

African Memories

Machine pieced, appliquéd, and quilted, hand embellished using African fabrics, beads, and wooden figures; 71 by 52-1/2 in. Photo: Mike Brown Photography, Seattle.

The design is a result of a lifetime of reading and studying about Africa and of a dream to travel there.

B

CAROL DRUMMOND
UNITED STATES

Sanctum

Hand and machine appliqué and piecing, hand quilting and embellishing on painted fabric; 32 by 36 in. Photo: Richard Drummond.

This piece is about longing for an inward place to go where there is no pain.

A

B

C

O DETTE T OLKSDORF
S OUTH A FRICA

It was hot when I arrived in Durban

Machine pieced, hand appliquéd, quilted, and embroidered cotton; 54 by 66 in.

D

S USAN S HIE AND J AMES A CORD
U NITED S TATES

The World of the Wondrous - A Green Quilt

Hand and machine appliquéd, embroidered, and quilted painted and embellished fabric; 75 by 72 in. Photo: Photography Unlimited.

This was commissioned by a family in New York City. It reflects their love of nature and the closeness of the parents and their son.

E

G RETCHEN E CHOLS
U NITED S TATES

Bob & Rita Try to Forget

Heat transfer, appliqué, machine piecing and quilting on commercial fabrics; 96 by 48 in. Photo: William Wickett.

We try to communicate with each other, but much is garbled and backward. We forget much of what we have learned about ourselves and each other as we focus on the mundane in our daily lives. We try and try again to live fuller lives but, alas, we manage to forget time and again the painful lessons we have learned.

E

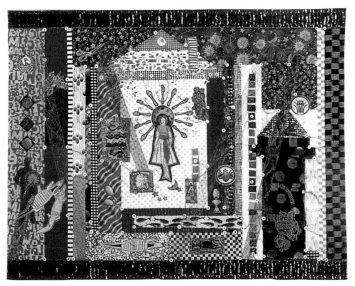

A

NANCY N. ERICKSON
UNITED STATES

The Gathering

Appliquéd, machine stitched, and painted satin, cotton, and velvet; 60 by 60-1/4 in.

Blackfoot Indian chief, Earl Old Person, said "every gathering is important."

B

JIM S. SMOOTE II
UNITED STATES

Modesty

Piecing, painting, and quilting on cotton; 50 by 41 in.

The figures represent a fetish or similar idealized male figure; the border is based on mud cloth.

C

JOYCE HYAM
AUSTRALIA

Pipe to the Spirit - After Dorrit Black

Machine pieced, appliquéd, and quilted hand dyed cotton; 86 by 122 cm.

My inspiration for this quilt is a black-and-white reproduction of a woodblock print by Dorrit Black.

A

C

B

D

D

CYNTHIA NIXON
UNITED STATES

Crash Quilt

Pieced, painted, appliquéd, and quilted cotton, satin, and silk; 38 by 40 in.

In a car accident in 1992, my dog was killed and my back was broken. I somehow experienced an incredible feeling of calm amid the chaos.

E

KATHRYN PELLMAN
UNITED STATES

Gang Bait

Machine appliquéd and quilted cotton; 120 by 90 in. Photo: Sharon Risedorph.

E

219

A

URSULA RAUCH
GERMANY

Inquisition

Batik, appliqué, embroidery, hand and machine quilting on cotton; 163 by 110 cm.

Since I have a background in painting and sculpture, my textile work is influenced by both.

B

JULIA E. PFAFF
UNITED STATES

#109, Why Have We Come Here?/Dashur

Hand and machine quilted, printed, and embroidered dyed and painted cotton; 84 by 61 in. Photo: Taylor Dabney.

My work is inspired by my experiences of the past 13 years of being an archaeological technical artist in Greece, Egypt, and Jordan. This is based on the site of Dashur, Egypt, where I worked 30 feet underground drawing royal tombs.

A

B

C

CAROLYN L. MAZLOOMI
UNITED STATES

The Family

Reverse appliquéd, hand painted and quilted cotton; 60 by 70 in.

Inspired by a linocut print, I wanted to celebrate the strength of the African-American family.

D

JANE REEVES
UNITED STATES

Tiger Rag

Machine pieced, hand appliquéd and quilted hand dyed and commercial cotton; 76 by 64 in.

E

ANNE TRIGUBA
UNITED STATES

Mandala

Hand appliquéd and quilted, machine pieced cotton; 65 by 65 in; quilting by Tomoko Takahashi.

C

D

E

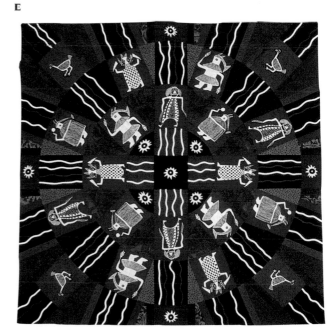

A

KATY J. WIDGER
UNITED STATES

Pinatubo: Fire in the Sky

Machine pieced and quilted,
hand appliquéd, painted, dyed,
and printed cotton; 51 by 50 in.
Photo: Ken Widger.

*The summer after the Pinatubo vol-
canic eruption in the Philippines,
sunsets near my central New Mexico
home were even more spectacular than
usual.*

B

URSULA KÖNIG
SWITZERLAND

Shallow Waters

Machine patchwork and quilting on silk and cotton; 150 by
120 cm.

*The sparkle of light on the rippling
surfaces of lakes impels me to duplicate it in fabric.*

A

B

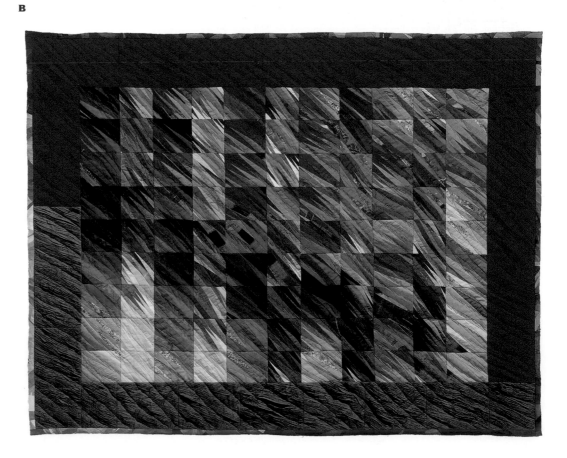

C

C

ERIKA CARTER
UNITED STATES

Parameters: Window

Machine appliquéd and quilted hand painted cotton and silk organza; 58 by 58 in. Photo: Ken Wagner.

The window is a metaphor for change, a bridge between the inside and outside, a threshold.

D

JEAN NEBLETT
UNITED STATES

Abstraction I: Separate Lives

Appliqué and machine quilted hand dyed cotton; 38 by 37 in. Photo: David Belda.

This was worked intuitively, with folded, torn, rolled, and stuffed fabric.

D

A

C ARYL B RYER
F ALLERT
U NITED S TATES

Flying Free

Machine pieced and quilted
hand dyed cotton; 22 by 22 in.

*Flying represents freedom to me. This
is the first in a series exploring the
idea of flights of the imagination.*

B

M ICHAEL J AMES
U NITED S TATES

Roundabout

Machine pieced and quilted
cotton and silk; 77 in. diameter.
Photo: David Caras.

A

B

C

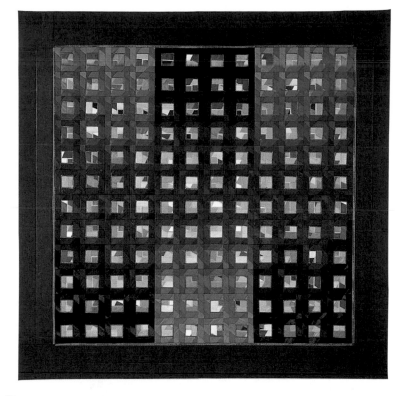

D

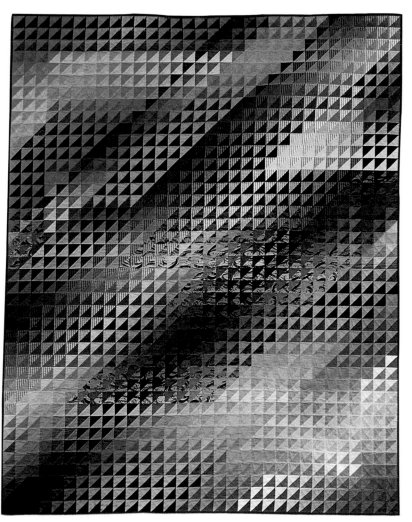

C

Schnuppe von Gwinner
Germany

Wassily's Colours

Patchwork technique using silk and cotton; 150 by 150 cm.

When this piece was finished, I hung it on the wall in my studio next to a poster of a Wassily Kandinsky painting. The composition of colours was similar, and so the title became obvious.

D

Mary Morgan
United States

To Make the Wind Visible

Machine pieced and quilted hand dyed cotton; 66 by 84 in.

Someone wrote that Christo's "Running Curtain" made the wind visible. This is my tribute to Christo, who just may be the ultimate fiber artist.

225

A

LINDA FOWLER
UNITED STATES

In Paradisum V

Machine appliquéd and quilted cotton and cotton blends; 45 by 45 in. Photo: Kevin Fitzsimons.

My intention was to draw upon the vegetation and life I saw in Guatemala. The piece took on a more personal meaning, though, and I just let it flow.

B

JANET ROBINSON
UNITED STATES

Prickly Heat © 1993

Machine pieced and quilted cotton, some hand dyed; 52 by 68 in. Photo: John Bonath.

At present, I am focusing on colors and how they interact. I try to be free and intuitive with my choices, letting the design grow and change as I play with the fabrics.

A

B

C

D

E

C

JANE A. SASSAMAN
UNITED STATES

Night Garden

Machine pieced, appliquéd, and quilted cotton, cotton blends, and lame; 61 by 63 in. Photo: Gregory Gantner.

D

LINDA S. PERRY
UNITED STATES

Night Person II

Hand appliqué, machine piecing and quilting of hand dyed cotton and rayon; 40 by 54 in. Photo: Joe Ofria.

My work reflects my interests in Japanese design and Art Deco.

E

CHARLOTTE YDE
DENMARK

Landscape of Memories

Hand appliquéd, machine pieced and quilted dyed cotton and silk; 140 by 150 cm. Photo: Dennis Rosenfeldt.

This was made to commemorate a very dear friend who died in 1993. Making the quilt helped me work through my grief.

A

LORI J. WILCOX
UNITED STATES

Implosion

Marbled, machine pieced, and hand quilted cotton; 40 by 28-1/4 in. Photo: Emile A. Corriveau.

B

JO AVERY
SCOTLAND

Sun Wheel Mandala - A Green Quilt

Piecing, appliqué, quilting, embroidery, and batik of cotton and wool; 49 by 49 in. Photo: Jonathan Avery.

Though intended to be a wall hanging, this quilt will still keep one warm at night.

C

PAMELA HILL
AUSTRALIA

Evensong

Hand and machine piecing, hand quilting, and "sashiko" stitching of cotton and silk; 15-1/2 by 19 in. Photo: Mark Lee.

One quilt is mounted upon another. The smaller of the two, inspired by the traditional cathedral window, seemed to have an inner harmony that was almost audible. When it was placed with its companion quilt, I could hear the choir.

D

JUDITH L. GEIGER
UNITED STATES

The Day God Looked Away

Machine pieced and quilted hand dyed cotton and silk; 20 by 16 by 1 in.

This is a commemoration of the survival of a family as Hurricane Andrew ripped apart the fabric of our world in Florida.

E

DONNA J. KATZ
UNITED STATES

Caribbean Star Chart

Hand painted and quilted, machine pieced muslin; 62 by 50 in.

My view of nature is both a concrete thing and a state of mind. I use imagery that portrays journeys that are emotional as well as physical.

A

B

C

D

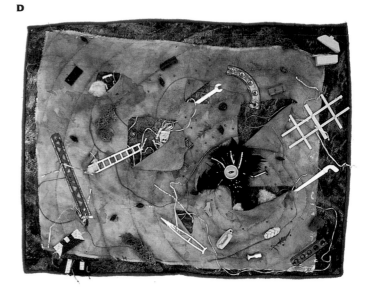

E

229

A

L Y N N E S W A R D
UNITED STATES

Home

Machine and hand appliquéd
and embroidered, machine
quilted cotton and blended
fabric; 48 by 38 in. Photo:
Michele Tillander.

*This piece began after I was day-
dreaming about a house on the water.*

B

K A R E N N . S O M A
UNITED STATES

Solar Palette

Hand dyed and screen printed,
machine pieced, quilted, and
embroidered cotton; 75 by 52
in. Photo: Bill Wickett.

*I am fascinated by the variations possi-
ble with even a simple design, and how
complex it can become if manipulated
and explored fully. To me, this speaks
to the unique possibilities each individual has while still bearing the basic
structure of every other human being.*

C

M A R Y M A S H U T A
UNITED STATES

Dawn for a New Day

Machine pieced and quilted
African fabrics; 77 by 77 in.
Photo: Sharon Risedorph.

*I taught quiltmaking in South Africa.
This quilt was made to commemorate
the democratic elections there, and to
celebrate the new direction the country
is taking.*

D

C A T H E R I N E W H A L L
S M I T H
UNITED STATES

Thirty-nine Rope Jumpers

Machine appliquéd and hand
quilted cotton; 71 by 72 in.
Photo: Jeff Burnham.

*The piece has just 38 squares of rope
jumpers, but the gold ropes appliquéd
to the quilt are an invitation to the
viewer to join in and, thus, become the
39th jumper.*

A

B

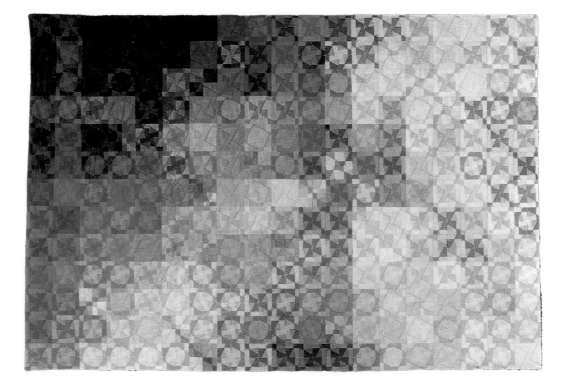

E

A N N E - M A R I E
S T E W A R T
E N G L A N D

Reverberations - Pink

Machine piecing and quilting, hand appliqué, tie-dyeing, and painting of cotton; 45-1/2 by 45-1/2 in. Photo: Richard Stewart.

This is from a series exploring color values. The idea came from school-based work with scissors, paper, and glue—taking a shape and exploding it into different patterns.

F

J I L L P A C E
U N I T E D S T A T E S

Free Spirit

Machine pieced, hand quilted, embroidered, and quilted cotton; 60 by 60 in.

C

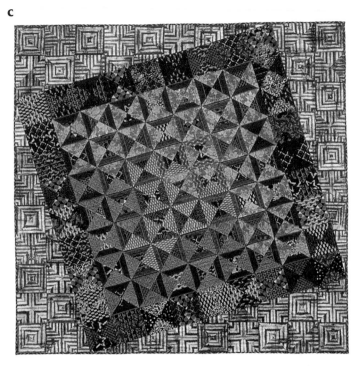

D

E

F

A

ETHEL SHULAM
UNITED STATES

Mimi's Marigold Patch

Machine pieced, quilted, and
embroidered silkscreened and
dyed cotton; 69 by 45-1/2 in.
Photo: David Caras.

B

KATHLEEN DENERIS
UNITED STATES

The Promise

Dyed, silkscreened, pieced,
appliquéd, quilted, and embroidered silk, rayon, and cotton; 66
by 48 in.

*A quilt can only capture the surface of
an experience or belief, and we have so
many. I like to think that a quilt is
like my life, where each day is joined
to another to make a larger story.*

C

GRETCHEN B. HILL
UNITED STATES

Shazam

Machine pieced and quilted
cotton; 80-1/4 by 64 in. Photo:
Tom Yarrish.

D

LIBBY LEHMAN
UNITED STATES

Escapade

Machine pieced, embroidered,
and quilted cotton; 81 by 81 in.
Collection of American Quilter's
Society, Peducah, Kentucky.

E

ELIZABETH
HENDRICKS
UNITED STATES

Chains

Machine pieced and quilted
cotton; 80 by 60 in. Photo: Ken
Wagner.

*This quilt evolved from a technique
taught by Margaret Miller.*

A

B

C

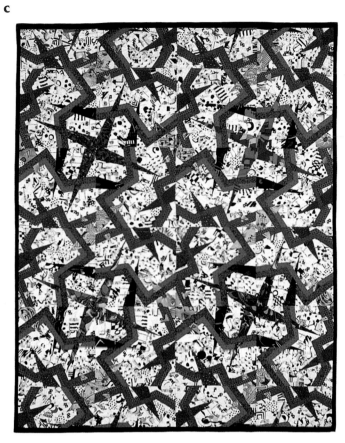

D

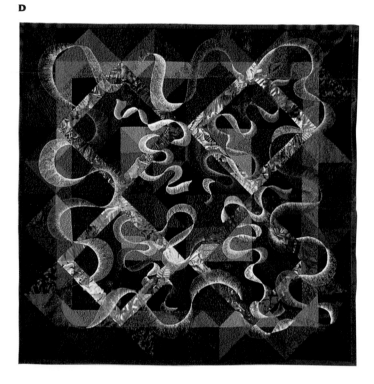

E

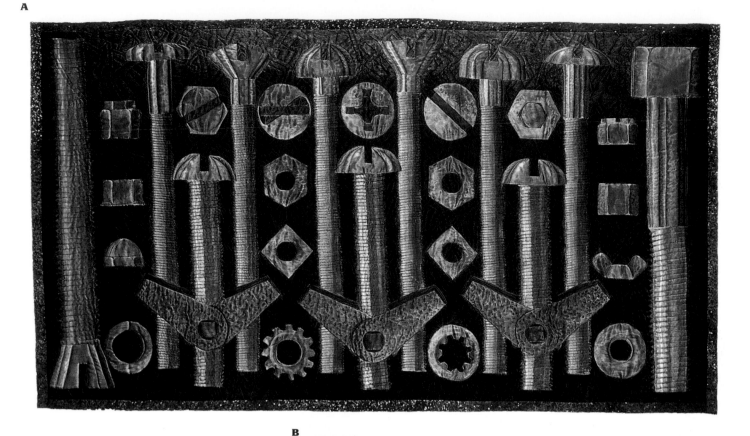

A

B

A

MARILYN L. HARRISON
UNITED STATES

Bolts of Cloth

Dye-painted, hand and machine quilted satin; 74 by 43 in.

I learned to appreciate the beauty of machine parts from my first boss who taught me the difference between toggle bolts and cotter pins so that I could prepare artwork for U.S. Army field manuals.

B

SOLFRID MEEK AL-KASIM
NORWAY

Nordic Spring II

Crazy patchwork, quilting, and machine embroidery of silk and cotton; 137 by 157 cm. Photo: Farouk Al-Kasim.

I began making quilts in 1978 when my husband brought 2,000 pieces of two-by-two-inch silk squares back from Thailand. What else could I possibly have done?

Ann Schumacher

INDEX

A

Magdalena Abakanowicz 14
Warsaw, Poland

Jackie Abrams 121
Groton, Vermont

Sophie Acheson 192
Greens Farms, Connecticut

James Acord 217
Wooster, Ohio

Sandy Adair 180
Boone, North Carolina

Ann M. Adams 206
San Antonio, Texas

Pat Adams 114
Saskatoon, Saskatchewan,
Canada

Renie Breskin Adams 78, 143
DeKalb, Illinois

Carol Adleman 41
Coon Rapids, Minnesota

Solfrid Meek Al-Kasim 234
Stavanger, Norway

Heather Allen 112
Smithville, Tennessee

Jane Ingram Allen 140
Hamilton, New York

Chris Allen-Wickler 44
Rochester, Minnesota

Irina Alova 173
St. Petersburg, Russia

Caroline Anderson 109
Nashville, Tennessee

Astrid Andreasen 75
Faroe Islands, Denmark

Jenniffer L. Andrzejewski 142
South Milwaukee, Wisconsin

Clare Arends 197
Hitchin, England

Kerstin Asling-Sundberg 105
Goteborg, Sweden

Janet Austin 168
Wakefield, Rhode Island

Jo Avery 228
Berwickshire, Scotland

Ilze Aviks 24
Durango, Colorado

B

Suzel Back 21
Montreal, Quebec, Canada

Lee Bale 46
Ashland, Oregon

Kathleen Baleja 95
Dauphin, Manitoba, Canada

Maribeth Baloga 77
Van Nuys, California

Deborah Banyas 146
Oberlin, Ohio

Cyndy Barbone 103
Greenwich, New York

Catherine Barritt 105
Alton, New Hampshire

Flo Barry 112
Houston, Texas

Carolyn Prince Batchelor 190
Upland, California

Judy Becker 206
Newton, Massachusetts

Kristina Becker 210
Pleasanton, California

Pamela E. Becker 41
Flemington, New Jersey

Linda L. Behar 79
Lexington, Massachusetts

Betsy Sterling Benjamin 20
Kyoto, Japan

Astrid Hilger Bennett 27
Iowa City, Iowa

Yael Bentovim 189
Los Angeles, California

Mary Bero 79
Madison, Wisconsin

Anne-Marie Bertand 98
Palaiseau, France

Karin Birch 74
Brunswick, Maryland

Lois Blackburn 108
Manchester, England

Cecilia Blomberg 183
Gig Harbor, Washington

Rebecca Bluestone 153
Santa Fe, New Mexico

Ilse Bolle 123
Palatine, Illinois

Jenifer A. Borg 21
Athens, Georgia

Dana Boussard 37
Arlee, Montana

George-Ann Bowers 160
Berkeley, California

Odette Brabec 165
Highland Park, Illinois

David B. Brackett 99
New Bethlehem, Pennsylvania

Barbara Brandel 60
Tucson, Arizona

Janet Carija Brandt 108
Indianapolis, Indiana

Ita Sadar Breznik 140
Ljubljana, Slovenia

Marla Brill 131
Highland Park, Illinois

Barbara Shaw Brinson 127
Laurens, South Carolina

Sue Broad 68
Palmerston North, New Zealand

Liese Bronfenbrenner 42
Ithaca, New York

Rachel Brumer 145
Seattle, Washington

Annemarie Duchmann Gerber 106
Saskatoon, Saskatchewan,
Canada

Elizabeth J. Buckley 183
Albuquerque, New Mexico

Anna Buczkowska 166
Konstancin, Poland

Carol Burns 73
Bloomsburg, Pennsylvania

Jeanne Lyons Butler 215
Huntington, New York

C

Dorothy Caldwell 42
Hastings, Ontario, Canada

Kay Campbell 24
Corvallis, Oregon

Joyce Marquess Carey 147
Madison, Wisconsin

Anna Carlson 47
Minneapolis, Minnesota

Erika Carter 223
Bellevue, Washington

Nick Cave 67
Chicago, Illinois

Debra Chase 137
New York, New York

Gerry Chase 204
Seattle, Washington

Judy Chicago 174-75
Albuquerque, New Mexico

Jenny Chippindale 27
Kettering, England

Peggotty Christensen 53
Phoenix, Arizona

Olga Dvigoubsky Cinnamon 138
Upland, California

Lisa Clark 22
Burnsville, North Carolina

Susan Clark 110
Saskatoon, Saskatchewan,
Canada

Morgan Elizabeth Clifford 97
St. Paul, Minnesota

Jane Burch Cochran 214
Rabbit Hash, Kentucky

Akemi Nakano Cohn 26
Chicago, Illinois

Laura F. Cohn 27
Bala Cynwyd, Pennsylvania

Cresside Collette 186
Balwyn, Victoria, Australia

Liza Collins 164
Leigh on Sea, England

Susie Colquitt 132
Marquette, Michigan

Heather Connelly 35
Merseyside, England

Joanell Connolly 57
Huntington Beach, California

Tricia Coulson 29
Ashland, Oregon

Audrey Cowan 174-75
Los Angeles, California

Barbara Crane 208
Lexington, Massachusetts

Nancy Crasco 209
Arlington, Massachusetts

Gloria E. Crouse 116
Olympia, Washington

Jackie Peters Cully 63
Huntington Station, New York

Michael A. Cummings 215
New York, New York

Margaret Cusack 116
Brooklyn, New York

Wlodzimierz Cygan 98
Lodz, Poland

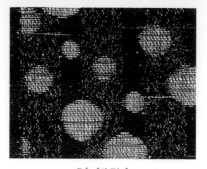

Bhakti Ziek

D

Diana Dabinett 20
Torbay, Newfoundland, Canada

Carolyn A. Dahl 57
Houston, Texas

Gina D'Ambrosio 49
Socorro, New Mexico

Maria Danielova 86
Prague, Czech Republic

Kay Henning Danley 35
Portland, Oregon

Marie-Jose Danzon 205
Toronto, Ontario, Canada

Heidi Darr-Hope 135
Columbia, South Carolina

Virginia Davis 101
New York, New York

Kathleen Deneris 232
Midvale, Utah

Linda Denier 149
Roselle, Illinois

Allison Dennis 69
Russellville, Kentucky

Martha Desposito 35
Chagrin Falls, Ohio

Nicole Dextras 195
Vancouver, British Columbia,
Canada

Maude Diggs 48
Corrales, New Mexico

Laurie Dill-Kocher 92
Rochester, New York

Mary F. Donovan 179
San Francisco, California

Sondra L. Dorn 25
Roxbury, Vermont

Carol Drummond 216
Sarasota, Florida

Jane Dunnewold 196
San Antonio, Texas

Christie L. Dunning 90
LaJolla, California

Herve Dupont 83
Etouy, France

Jennifer Dyer 125
Condon, Montana

Tony Dyer 38
Moone Ponds, Victoria,
Australia

Noel Dyrenforth 30
London, England

E

Gretchen Echols 217
Seattle, Washington

Ellen Anne Eddy 144
Chicago, Illinois

Jilly Edwards 177
Kendal, England

Lore Edzard 177
Nashville, Tennessee

Sylvia H. Einstein 212
Belmont, Massachusetts

Alexa Elam 148
Richmond, Virginia

Theodora Elston 76, 161
Sonoma, California

Nancy N. Erickson 218
Missoula, Montana

Phyllis Ceratto Evans 90
Bainbridge Island, Washington

Suzanne Evenson 207
Worthington, Ohio

F

Isabelle Faidy-Contreau 84
Montmorillion, France

Caryl Bryer Fallert 224
Oswego, Illinois

Leslie Nobler Farber 95
Demarest, New Jersey

Carola Farthing 127
Mill Valley, California

Barbara P. Fast 191
Harrisonburg, Virginia

Judith Poxson Fawkes 102
Portland, Oregon

Felicia 80
La Croix Valmer, France

Mario Alberto Fernandez 133
Buenos Aires, Argentina

Maria Luisa Ferreira 181
Lisbon, Portugal

Cristina Ferrer 182
Buenos Aires, Argentina

Martha Ferris 26
Vicksburg, Mississippi

Maria Assunta Forster
Ferrugem 200
Porto Alegre, Brazil

Diane Bevan Fields 107
Hickory, North Carolina

Pia Filliger-Nolte 70
Rodinghausen, Germany

Donna M. Fleming 24
Durango, Colorado

Paula K. Foresman 207
Mansfield, Massachusetts

Linda Fowler 226
Columbus, Ohio

Molly R.M. Fowler 200
West Hartford, Connecticut

Mollie Freeman 70
Sacramento, California

Suzan Friedland 204
San Francisco, California

Alexandra S. Friedman 170
Hartford, Connecticut

Paul Friedman 62
Olivebridge, New York

W. Logan Fry 101
Richfield, Ohio

G

Gail Gagnon-Garcia 55
Redlands, California

Eva Gallant 196
Edgartown, Massachusetts

Ruth Garrison 211
Tempe, Arizona

Anja Gartzke 198
Elmenhorst, Germany

Fiona Gavens 213
Whiteman Creek, New South
Wales, Australia

Stela Gazzaneo 62
Porto Alegre, Brazil

Judith L. Geiger 229
Jupiter, Florida

Leslie Christine Gelber 58
Auburn, California

Peter Gentenaar 132
Rijswijk, The Netherlands

Pat Gentenaar-Torley 194
Rijswijk, The Netherlands

Ursula Gerber-Senger 75
Mannedorf, Switzerland

Murray Gibson 165
London, England

Roberta Glidden 28
Ogden, Utah

Anne Glum 50
Berlin, Germany

Jeannine Goreski 121
Tucson, Arizona

Kirsty Gorter 84
Broadmeadows, Victoria,
Australia

Jacqueline Govin 93
Fontaine/Jouy, France

Tim Gresham 187
Hawthorne, Victoria, Australia

Joan Griffin 182
Hammondsport, New York

Michalene Groshek 136
Hartland, Wisconsin

Schnuppe von Gwinner 225
Hamburg, Germany

H

Chad Alice Hagen 198
St. Paul, Minnesota

Joan Hall 202
St. Louis, Missouri

Jan Hamilton 64
London, England

Jenny Hansen 187
Aabybro, Denmark

Ellen Harlizius-Kluck 43
Neuss, Germany

Kaija Sanelma Harris 154
Saskatoon, Saskatchewan,
Canada

Peter Harris 183
Ayton, Ontario, Canada

Marilyn L. Harrison 234
Boca Raton, Florida

David Hartge 52, 55
Brookeville, Maryland

Linda France Hartge 52, 55
Brookeville, Maryland

Ann Hartley 87
Houston, Texas

Patty Hawkins 214
Lyons, Colorado

Ana Lisa Hedstrom 9, 10
Emeryville, California

Sheila Held 179
Wauwarosa, Wisconsin

Barbara Heller 160
Vancouver, British Columbia,
Canada

Lynne Heller 205
Toronto, Ontario, Canada

Priscilla Henderson 122
Lake Forest, Illinois

Elizabeth Hendricks 233
Seattle, Washington

Maggie Henton 129
London, England

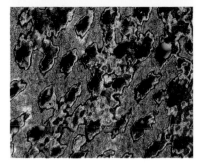

Karen S. Page

Helena Hernmarck 15
Ridgefield, Connecticut

Silvia Heyden 157
San Nazzaro, Switzerland

Cindy Hickok 143
Houston, Texas

Gretchen B. Hill 233
San Jose, California

Pamela Hill 229
Brisbane, Queensland,
Australia

Betty Hilton-Nash 185
Little River, California

Cecilia Hjelm 25
Goteborg, Sweden

Marjorie Hoeltzel 191
St. Louis, Missouri

Catherine Hoffmann 185
Warrnambool, Victoria,
Australia

Cas Holmes 197
Maidstone, England

Kathleen Holmes 89
Lake Worth, Florida

Mimi Holmes 138
Minneapolis, Minnesota

Susan Holmes 66
Devonport, Auckland, New
Zealand

Melissa Holzinger 37
Arlington, Washington

Hoop 150
Clifton, New Jersey

Flo Hoppe 120
Rome, New York

Sara Hotchkiss 176
Portland, Maine

Shirley How 34
Richmond, California

Kim Huber 53
Louisville, Kentucky

Holly Hughes 150
Socorro, New Mexico

Ellen J. Hutchinson 65
St. Paul, Minnesota

Fiona R. Hutchison 186
Edinburgh, Scotland

Joyce Hyam 218
Brisbane, Queensland,
Australia

I

Marie-Laure Ilie 30
Redondo Beach, California

Peg Irish 111
Waquoit, Massachusetts

Diane Itter 15
Deceased

Susan Iverson 175
Richmond, Virginia

J

Anne Jackson 148
Crediton, England

Lorraine Jackson 62
Olivebridge, New York

Victor Jacoby 164
Eureka, California

Lucy A. Jahns 18
Vernon Hills, Illinois

Karen Olesen Jakse 96
Eden Prairie, Minnesota

Feliksas Jakubauskas 158
Vilnius, Lithuania

Lois James 191
Palos Verdes, California

Michael James 224
Somerset Village,
Massachusetts

Jan Janas 17
Boulder, Colorado

Jan Janeiro 135
El Prado, New Mexico

I. Wojciech Jaskolka 96
Krakow, Poland

Anne S. Jennings 85
Salt Lake City, Utah

Rosita Johanson 135, 143
Toronto, Ontario, Canada

Jodi Johnston 164
Denver, Colorado

Raija Jokinen 197
Helsinki, Finland

Arnout Jongejan 162
Carp, Ontario, Canada

Zilvinas Jonutis 159
Vilnius, Lithuania

K

Jodi Kanter 134
Lyndhurst, Ohio

Marcia Karlin 33
Lincolnshire, Illinois

Donna J. Katz 229
Chicago, Illinois

Ann Keister 153
Bloomington, Indiana

Rose Kelly 64
Oakland, California

Lori Kemp 146
Black Mountain, North Carolina

Lois Kennedy-Paine 168
Gibsons, British Columbia,
Canada

Anne Marie Kenny 89
Hooksett, New Hampshire

Jane Kenyon 50
Bowen Island, British
Columbia, Canada

Jane Kidd 115
Calgary, Alberta, Canada

Anne Kinkaid 72
Seattle, Washington

Geri Kinnear 207
Hinsdale, Illinois

Valerie Kirk 159
Downer, Capital Territory,
Australia

Barbara Klaer 54
Amesville, Ohio

Judith Klaer-Kerns 54
Amesville, Ohio

Susanne Klinke 77
Meschede, Germany

Katherine Knauer 94
New York, New York

Sally Knight 128
Burlington, Vermont

Rebecca Clark Knudsen 111
Provo, Utah

Ursula Konig 222
Ostermundigen, Switzerland

Dobroslawa Kowalewska 82
Lodz, Poland

Kathleen Peelen Krebs 120
Berkeley, California

Tracy Krumm Cover, 192
Oakland, California

Lialia Kuchma 177
Chicago, Illinois

Janet Kuemmerlein 128
Prairie Village, Kansas

Elizabeth G. Kuhn 105
Kent, Ohio

Sharon Phipps Kump 194
Garden Grove, California

Franziska Kurth 178
Berlin, Germany

L

Catherine La Du 44
Ann Arbor, Michigan

Linda Laino 201
Richmond, Virginia

Mary Catherine Lamb 90
Portland, Oregon

Edward S. Lambert 31
Athens, Georgia

Elisabet Lamm 37
Vanersborg, Sweden

Mary Lane 163
Olympia, Washington

Ruth E. Lantz 61
Columbus, Ohio

Nina Laptchik 184
Kiev, Ukraine

Jean Pierre Larochette 181
Berkeley, California

Ulrika Leander 169
Oak Ridge, Tennessee

Patti Lechman 119
Memphis, Tennessee

Chunghie Lee 51
Seoul, Korea

Claudia Lee 195
Kingsport, Tennessee

Susan Webb Lee 207
Weddington, North Carolina

Connie Lehman 72
Elizabeth, Colorado

Libby Lehman 233
Houston, Texas

Rita P. Lenn 52
East Setauket, New York

Susan Leopold 196
Toronto, Ontario, Canada

Janet Leszczynski 78
Glencoe, Illinois

Marc Leuthold 9
New York, New York

Linda Levin 36
Wayland, Massachusetts

Mina Levitan-Babenskiene 187
Vilnius, Lithuania

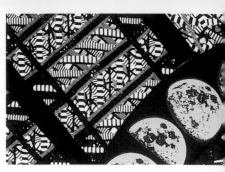

Greg Somerville

Linda Lewis 73
  Tempe, Arizona

Bojana H. Leznicki 154
  Verona, New Jersey

Erica Licea-Kane 134
  Arlington, Massachusetts

Lore Lindenfeld 93
  Princeton, New Jersey

Margot Lindsay 79
  Saskatoon, Saskatchewan,
  Canada

Milissa Link 83
  Minneapolis, Minnesota

M. Joan Lintault 31
  Carbondale, Illinois

Linda Livesey 201
  Lancaster, England

Birgitta Ljungberg 180
  Malmoe, Sweden

Roslyn Logsdon 109
  Laurel, Maryland

Lynne Lomofsky 29
  Toronto, Ontario, Canada

Kit Loney 92
  Folly Beach, South Carolina

Dona Look 118
  Algoma, Wisconsin

Doris Louie 151
  San Ysidro, New Mexico

Peggy Love 77
  Darien, Connecticut

Tom Lundberg 11, 81
  Ft. Collins, Colorado

Yael Lurie 181
  Berkeley, California

M

Linda R. MacDonald 45
  Willits, California

Margo Macdonald 172
  Vaughn, Washington

Gila Mader 83
  Upper Galilee, Israel

Irene Maginniss 190
  Mansfield, Ohio

Julianna Mahley 74
  Vienna, Virginia

Patricia Malarcher 94
  Englewood, New Jersey

Aleksandra Manczak 139
  Lodz, Poland

Carol McKie Manning 65
  San Marcos, California

Ruth Manning 169
  Rochester, New York

Sharon Marcus 155
  Portland, Oregon

Donna Rhae Marder 88
  Winchester, Massachusetts

Marcel Marois 155
  Quebec City, Quebec, Canada

Collis Caroline Marshall 72
  Louisville, Kentucky

Cherilyn Martin 212
  Nymegen, The Netherlands

Donna Martin 157
  Santa Fe, New Mexico

Heather Martin 56
  Sherston, England

Kate Martin 115
  Ojai, California

Tracy Martin 49
  Valdese, North Carolina

Nancy Martineau 108
  Marysville, Washington

Mary Mashuta 231
  Berkeley, California

Fuyuko Matsubara 106
  Syracuse, New York

Yoshiko Matsuda 23
  Savannah, Georgia

Prudence Matthews 110
  Binghamton, New York

Jean Matzke 80
  St. Cloud, Minnesota

Carolyn L. Mazloomi 221
  Cincinnati, Ohio

Elaine D. McBride 81
  Bridgewater, Massachusetts

Karen L. McCarthy 36
  Arlington, Massachusetts

John E. McGuire 130
  Geneva, New York

Katherine L. McKearn 144
  Towson, Maryland

Judith McNally-Warner 34
  Fabius, New York

NanC Meinhardt 59, 72
  Highland Park, Illinois

Kim Yost Merck 69
  Brunswick, Georgia

Mary Merkel-Hess 123
  Iowa City, Iowa

Ed Johnetta Miller 62
  Hartfield, Connecticut

Sergey Minaev 188
  St. Petersburg, Russia

Marjorie Mink 18
  Ann Arbor, Michigan

Norma Minkowitz 132
  Westport, Connecticut

Betsy R. Miraglia 192
  Radnor, Pennsylvania

Julia Mitchell 163
  Vineyard Haven, Massachusetts

Lesley Mitchison 99
  Stoke on Trent, England

Janice Moezzi 76
  Philadelphia, Pennsylvania

Kathleen Mollahan 184
  Helena, Montana

Gabriela Ortiz Monasterio 146
  Morelia, Mexico

Audrey Moore 171
  Sandy, Oregon

Janet Moore 179
  San Francisco, California

Marilyn Moore 118
  Seattle, Washington

Mary Morgan 225
  Little Rock, Arkansas

Judy Morningstar 95
  Dauphin, Manitoba, Canada

Anne Morrell 24
  Stockport, England

Lois Morrison 136
  Leonia, New Jersey

Zoe Morrow 125
  Pennsauken, New Jersey

Barbara J. Mortenson 33
  Glenside, Pennsylvania

Robyn Mountcastle 187
  Hawthorne, Victoria, Australia

Judy Mulford 125
  Los Angeles, California

Clare M. Murray 42
  Canton, Ohio

Diane Muse 144
  Towson, Maryland

Aina Muze 173
  Riga, Latvia

N

Dominie Nash 40
  Bethesda, Maryland

Karin Nebel 107
  Basel, Switzerland

Jean Neblett 223
  San Francisco, California

Charlene K. Nemec 91
  Chicago, Illinois

Darlene Nguyen-Ely 122
  Long Beach, California

Sandra Gayle Nickeson 73
  St. Louis, Missouri

Anne McKenzie Nickolson 82
  Indianapolis, Indiana

Lene Nielsen 54
  Aars, Denmark

Cynthia Nixon 219
  State College, Pennsylvania

Beth Nobles 78, 81
  Riverside, Iowa

Inge Norgaard 174
  Port Townsend, Washington

Vlasta Novakova 158
  Prague, Czech Republic

O

Lindsay Obermeyer 93
  Chicago, Illinois

Sheila O'Hara 149, 171
  Oakland, California

Martha Donovan Opdahl 113
  Greencastle, Indiana

P

Jill Pace 231
  Glendale, Arizona

Karen S. Page 199
  Beaver Falls, Pennsylvania

Andra Panduru 166
  Bucharest, Romania

Rosita Pardo 53
  Richmond, California

Hyang Sook Park 32
  Seoul, Korea

Soyoo Hyunjoo Park 155, 185
  Closter, New Jersey

Jill N. Parker-Trotter 145
  Chicago, Illinois

Jacque Parsley 142
  Louisville, Kentucky

Cherry Partee 44
Edmonds, Washington

Pam Patrie 163
Portland, Oregon

Junanne Peck 63
Dallas, Texas

Whitney J. Peckman 161
Friday Harbor, Washington

Kathryn Pellman 219
Los Angeles, California

Ulric Paul Pereira 52
Scarborough, Ontario, Canada

Fran Gardner Perry 23
Lancaster, South Carolina

Linda S. Perry 227
Lexington, Massachusetts

Jacques Pete 19
Dijon, France

Julia E. Pfaff 18, 220
Richmond, Virginia

Lyn Pierre 194
Albuquerque, New Mexico

Judith Pinnell 58
Dalkeith, Western Australia,
Australia

Gwynn Popovac 67
Sonora, California

David C. Powers 138
Damascus, Maryland

Suzanne Pretty 170
Farmington, New Hampshire

Donna Prichard 147
Bellevue, Washington

Nancy Prichard 193
Virginia Beach, Virginia

Sylvia Ptak 133
Toronto, Ontario, Canada

Ricki C. Pucke 150
Cincinnati, Ohio

Liz Pulos 104
Burlington, Vermont

Valerija Purlyte 156
Vilnius, Lithuania

R

Bill Rafnel 116
Vista, California

Lija Rage 156
Riga, Latvia

Nel Rand 108
Manning, Oregon

Ursula Rauch 220
Weingarten, Germany

Marilyn Rea-Menzies 168
Christchurch, New Zealand

Jane Reeves 221
Canton, Ohio

Camille Remme 210
Toronto, Ontario, Canada

Gabrielle Rensch 61
Sackville, New Brunswick,
Canada

Ruth Reynolds 144
Joliet, Illinois

Ann Richards 70
London, England

Emily Richardson 43
Philadelphia, Pennsylvania

Wendy Richardson 51
Brooklyn Park, Minnesota

Kathleen Richert 64
Stillwater, Minnesota

Nanilee S. Robarge 45
San Francisco, California

Janet Robinson 226
Highlands Ranch, Colorado

Sharon Robinson 124
Santa Rosa, California

Letitia Kaminski Roller 167
Lima, Ohio

Bird Ross 56, 124
Madison, Wisconsin

Ed Rossbach 13
Berkeley, California

Elaine Rounds 95
Dauphin, Manitoba, Canada

Kristin Carlsen Rowley 180
Iowa City, Iowa

Renata Rozsivalova 160
Prague, Czech Republic

Magda Rubalcava 157
Dublin, Ireland

Deann Rubin 167
Melrose, Massachusetts

Anatoly Rubtzov 188
St. Petersburg, Russia

Zuzana Rudavska 89
Brooklyn, New York

Tracy Ruhlin 23
Findlay, Ohio

Lu Rulai 186
Hangzhou, China

Mary Russell 66
San Luis Obispo, California

Fran Cutrell Rutkovsky 98
Tallahassee, Florida

Jeffrey T. Rutledge 133
Lexington, Kentucky

S

Linda K. Sage 61
Morgantown, Indiana

Ramona Sakiewstewa 175
Santa Fe, New Mexico

Teresa Graham Salt 171
Greenville, North Carolina

Paula J. Sarge 211
Midland, Michigan

Jane A. Sassaman 226
Chicago, Illinois

Jane Sauer 117
St. Louis, Missouri

Joy Saville 88
Princeton, New Jersey

Tommye McClure Scanlin 172
Dahlonega, Georgia

Lois Schklar 131
Thornhill, Ontario, Canada

Virginia J. Schlosser 216
Bellevue, Washington

Margrit Schmidtke 137
Millersville, Pennsylvania

Andrew Schneider 176
Kherson, Ukraine

Yuri Schneider 176
Kherson, Ukraine

Marie Schneider-Seniuk 188
Kherson, Ukraine

Barbara Schulman 107
Kutztown, Pennsylvania

Ann Schumacher 178
Berea, Kentucky

Alison Schwabe 212
Shelley, Western Australia,
Australia

Tilleke Schwarz 86
Pijnacker, The Netherlands

Sara L. Scott 56
Tempe, Arizona

Amanda Sears 113
Santa Cruz, California

Sally A. Sellers 91
Vancouver, Washington

Kathleen Sharp 203
Monte Sereno, California

Lisa Sharp 57
Houston, Texas

Marilyn Sharp 127
Black Mountain, North Carolina

Giselle Shepatin 69
San Francisco, California

Susan Shie 217
Wooster, Ohio

Ethel Shulam 232
Peabody, Massachusetts

Sandra Sider 40
Brooklyn, New York

Barbara Siedlecka 193
Beckenham, England

Anne de la Mauviniere Silva 209
Ottawa, Ontario, Canada

Louisa Simons 30
Ambleside, England

John I. Skau 114
Archdale, North Carolina

Elaine Small 142
Ferguson, Missouri

Ann Smith 27
Barnham, England

Catherine Whall Smith 231
Chaplin, Connecticut

Delores Darby Smith 22
Mercer Island, Washington

Elly Smith 84
Medina, Washington

Gloria Z. Smith 190
Cedar Rapids, Iowa

Nancy Smith 211
Littleton, Colorado

Jim S. Smoote II 218
Chicago, Illinois

Melinda Muhn Snyder 76
Louisville, Kentucky

Karen N. Soma 230
Seattle, Washington

Greg Somerville 28
Lawson, New South Wales,
Australia

Patricia H. Spark 201
Albany, Oregon

Elinor J. Splitter 119
Maitland, Florida

Maria J. Stachowska 199
Richmond, England

Karen Stahlecker 202
Anchorage, Alaska

Care Standley 178
Albany, California

Elaine McBride

Dianne Stanton 126
  Pembroke, Massachusetts

Cherie St. Cyr 48
  Madison, Wisconsin

Jo Stealey 121
  Columbia, Missouri

Elinor Steele 148, 173
  Middlebury, Vermont

Ethel Stein 8
  Croton-on-Hudson, New York

Oriane Stender 101
  San Francisco, California

Dorle Stern-Straeter 51, 213
  Munich, Germany

Anne-Marie Stewart 231
  Ipswich, England

Joy Stocksdale 54
  Berkeley, California

Brenda J. Stultz 105
  Fairmount, Illinois

Billie Ruth Sudduth 127
  Spruce Pine, North Carolina

Zia Sutherland 22
  Kinburn, Ontario, Canada

Catrina Sutter 103
  Russell, New Zealand

Margrit Sutter-Furrer 159
  St. Gallen, Switzerland

Lynne Sward 230
  Virginia Beach, Virginia

Karen James Swing 57
  Boone, North Carolina

T

Reni Tajima 128
  Tokyo, Japan

Noriko Takamiya 130
  Kanagawa, Japan

Keiko Takeda 129
  Tokyo, Japan

Mitsuko Tarui 199
  Tokyo, Japan

Cameron Taylor-Brown 104
  Los Angeles, California

Odette Tolksdorf 216
  Durban, South Africa

Marjorie Tomchuk 193
  New Canaan, Connecticut

Charlotte Torgovitsky 60
  San Rafael, California

Judith Trager 215
  Boulder, Colorado

Jacqueline Treloar 46
  Toronto, Ontario, Canada

Anne Triguba 221
  Lancaster, Ohio

Lori Johnson Turel 166
  Beaverton, Oregon

Jonni Turner 85
  Regina, Saskatchewan, Canada

Mary Tyler 28
  Kalamazoo, Michigan

U

Leslie Marie Ulrich 86
  Seattle, Washington

Bette Uscott-Woolsey 40
  Bala Cynwyd, Pennsylvania

V

Ray Varnbuhler 114
  Wilseyville, California

Betty Vera 102
  New York, New York

Meiny Vermaas-van der Heide 208
  Tempe, Arizona

Clare Verstegen 32
  Tempe, Arizona

Judith Vierow 145
  Columbus, Ohio

Chris Vietmeier 147
  St. Helens, Oregon

Vickie Vipperman 100
  Kingston Springs, Tennessee

Zinaida Vogeliene 167
  Vilnius, Lithuania

Christina Benson Vos 149
  Hoboken, New Jersey

W

Elizabeth Wadsworth-Mandell 39
  Bloomington, Indiana

Wendy Wahl 113
  West Kingston, Rhode Island

Mika Watanabe 139
  Brookline, Massachusetts

Mona Waterhouse 193
  Peachtree City, Georgia

Alice Watterson 141
  Phoenix, Arizona

Kathy Weaver 33
  Highland Park, Illinois

Helen Webb 126
  Darlington, England

Sandy Webster 63
  Brasstown, North Carolina

Zhu Wei 132
  Hangzhou, China

David Weidig 95
  Rancho Santa Margarita,
  California

Linda Welker 61
  Forest Grove, Oregon

Pat Weller 82
  Oakland, California

Carol Wilcox Wells 59
  Asheville, North Carolina

Melinda West 122
  Indianola, Washington

Marie Westerman 100
  Minneapolis, Minnesota

Carol D. Westfall 120
  Nutley, New Jersey

Margaret Roach Wheeler 66
  Joplin, Missouri

Jan Whitaker 110
  Haydenville, Massachusetts

Pamela Whitlock 68
  Asheville, North Carolina

Katy J. Widger 222
  Edgewood, New Mexico

Susan Wilchins 39
  Raleigh, North Carolina

Lori J. Wilcox 228
  Warwick, Rhode Island

Sandra Wiles 38
  Victoria, British Columbia,
  Canada

Gayle Williamson 79
  Louisville, Kentucky

Jeanne Williamson 39
  Natick, Massachusetts

Jay Wilson 152
  Maui, Hawaii

Ann Winterling 111
  Concord, New Hampshire

Sharmini Wirasekara 58
  North Vancouver, British
  Columbia, Canada

Char Wiss 118
  Washington, District of
  Columbia

Mariette Wolbert 107
  Purmerend, The Netherlands

Joan Wolfer 74
  Boulder, Colorado

Joanne Woll 48
  Florissant, Missouri

Natacha Wolters 59
  Berlin, Germany

Michele G. Wood 200
  Normal, Illinois

Y

Charlotte Yde 227
  Frederiksberg, Denmark

Hyun-Ah Yoo 21
  Seoul, Korea

Erma Martin Yost 45
  Jersey City, New Jersey

Iain Young 162
  Murrumbeena, Victoria,
  Australia

Z

Theodora Zehner 85
  Madison, Wisconsin

Mary Zena 130
  Louisville, Kentucky

Claire Zeisler 12
  Deceased

Mary Zicafoose 152
  Portland, Oregon

Bhakti Ziek 97
  Philadelphia, Pennsylvania

Christine Zoller 19
  Athens, Georgia